ONE FLEW OVER THE CUCKOO'S NEST

Ken Kesey

AUTHORED by Jeremy Ross
UPDATED AND REVISED by Soman Chainani, February 19, 2008, and
Adam Kissel,

COVER DESIGN by Table XI Partners LLC
COVER PHOTO by Olivia Verma and © 2005 GradeSaver, LLC

BOOK DESIGN by Table XI Partners LLC

Published by GradeSaver LLC, www.gradesaver.com

First published in the United States of America by GradeSaver LLC. 2000

GRADESAVER, the GradeSaver logo and the phrase "Getting you the grade
since 1999" are registered trademarks of GradeSaver, LLC

ISBN 978-1-60259-134-9

Printed in the United States of America

For other products and additional information please visit

Table of Contents

Table of Contents

Biography of Ken Kesey (1935-2001)

Ken Kesey, the older of two sons, was born on September 17, 1935, in La Junta, Colorado. In 1946 the family moved to Springfield, Oregon, where Kesey spent several years on his family's farm. He was raised in a religious household where he developed a great appreciation for Christian fables and a Christian ethical system. During high school and later in college, Kesey was a champion wrestler, setting long-standing state records in Oregon. Voted "most likely to succeed" in high school, Kesey was an unlikely candidate to become one of the more controversial figures of his age and one of the leading figures of the counterculture.

After high school, Kesey eloped with Faye Haxby, his high school sweetheart, and they had three children together: Jed, Zane, and Shannon. Kesey attended the University of Oregon with a degree in Speech and Communications. He also received a Woodrow Wilson Fellowship to enroll in the Creative Writing program at Stanford. His classmates in the program included Robert Stone, Larry McMurty, Ken Babbs, and Wendell Berry, all of whom would go on to be noted writers and lifelong friends of Kesey.

While at Stanford, he participated in government-funded experiments involving chemicals at the psychology department to earn extra money. These chemicals included psilocybin, mescaline, and LSD. This experience fundamentally altered Kesey, personally and professionally. While working as an orderly at the psychiatric ward of the local VA hospital, Kesey began to have hallucinations about an Indian sweeping the floors. This formed the basis for Chief Bromden (for "broom") in One Flew Over the Cuckoo's Nest, his writing project at Stanford.

At this time, Kesey lived at Perry Lane, a bohemian community in Palo Alto, where he became notorious for throwing parties in which certain chemicals mysteriously found their way into the punch. Kesey published One Flew Over the Cuckoo's Nest in 1962. The novel was an immediate critical and popular success. Dale Wasserman adapted it into a successful stage play, and Milos Forman directed a screen adaptation in 1975.

To do research for his second novel, which dealt with a family of loggers, Kesey moved to La Honda, California, in the redwood hills of San Mateo County. Surrounded by old friends from Perry Lane and similarly adventurous-minded travelers, La Honda became a de facto bohemian rural community. Writer Hunter S. Thompson remembered La Honda as "the world capital of madness. There were no rules, fear was unknown and sleep was out of the question." While Kesey and others had their families, they simultaneously experimented with all types of drugs, and every night seemed to bring a blowout party with the likes of Allen Ginsberg, the Hells Angels, and the weirdest outliers of San Francisco.

Despite the chaos at La Honda, Kesey managed to finish his second novel,

Sometimes a Great Notion (1964). The novel deals with the conflicts between West Coast individualism and East Coast intellectualism. In 1964, Kesey and his friends, who had become known as the Merry Pranksters, bought a 1939 International Harvest school bus and drove to New York to see the World's Fair. Kesey recruited Neal Cassady from Kerouac's On the Road to drive the bus. Kesey filmed a significant portion of the journey, and he later would show clips from the trip to chemically-induced audiences at his parties. Kesey became the proponent of a local band known as the "Warlocks," which later became the Grateful Dead.

Kesey and his Merry Pranksters became notorious for their "Acid Tests" and use of LSD and other drugs. Kesey's exploits with the Merry Pranksters during this period formed the basis for a best-selling book by Tom Wolfe (A Man in Full, The Bonfire of the Vanities) called The Electric Kool-Aid Acid Test. When the government made LSD illegal, Ken and the Pranksters fled to Mexico, where Kesey tried to fake a suicide in order to escape later prosecution. But when he returned to the United States for a final performance, he was arrested on a marijuana charge, leading to a five-month prison sentence at the San Mateo County Jail. Upon his release from jail, Kesey moved to a farm in Pleasant Hill, Oregon, with his wife to raise his four children. He quietly taught a graduate writing seminar at the University of Oregon.

Kesey published Kesey's Garage Sale in 1973. His later works include Little Tricker the Squirrel Meets Big Double the Bear, a children's book (1990); Sailor Song (1992); and Last Go Around (1994), his last book, about a famous rodeo in Oregon.

Decades after his counterculture experience, Kesey never settled down. As he attested on his website late in life, Kesey warned that every now and then he got the itch to do "something weird." Kesey died on November 10, 2001, following cancer surgery on his liver.

About One Flew Over the Cuckoo's Nest

One Flew Over the Cuckoo's Nest (1962) combines the personal and professional experiences of Ken Kesey and reflects the culture in which it was written, yet it stands strong on its own merits. Kesey developed the novel while a graduate student in Stanford University's Creative Writing Program. The novel was partly inspired by Kesey's part-time job as an orderly in the Palo Alto Menlo Park Veterans' Hospital. Kesey also had begun participating in experiments involving LSD and other substances for Stanford's Psychology Department. Speaking to patients under the influence of LSD, Kesey began to perceive that society had turned functional people insane instead of allowing them to find their way back to functioning in society. Kesey's use of LSD also prompted him to have hallucinations while working as an orderly. Kesey often imagined seeing a large Indian mopping the floors of the hospital, prompting him to later add the character of Chief Bromden as the novel's narrator.

Kesey published One Flew Over the Cuckoo's Nest to great critical and commercial success. Upon publication, the novel had a tremendous effect on baby boomers just beginning to awaken to stirrings of rebellion, for it mirrored and stirred up their new challenges to authority. Kesey also found himself financially relieved by the success of the novel, which allowed him to move his family to a large estate in La Honda, California, which became the site of his wildest days as a bohemian, partying with the likes of the Hells Angels, Allen Ginsberg, and San Francisco's hippest cultural figures.

The information that he included from his experiences at the veterans' hospital proved problematic; Kesey and his publisher, Viking Press, were sued by a plaintiff who claimed that a minor character in the novel, a Red Cross nurse, was based on her and that she was unfairly portrayed. The case resulted in revisions to subsequent editions of the book. The Red Cross nurse was changed to the nameless character Public Relation. The plaintiff in the case later became a novelist herself (and was later the subject of a defamation lawsuit).

In the context of the changing attitudes at the time, the novel in some sense forms a bridge between the bohemian beatnik movements of the 1950s and the counterculture movements of the 1960s. Kesey was significantly inspired by the beatnik culture around Stanford, and in the novel Kesey deals with a number of themes that would be significant in the counterculture movement, including notions of freedom from repressive authority and a more liberated view of sexuality. Kesey himself became a highly influential counterculture figure as part of a group known as the Merry Pranksters.

One Flew Over the Cuckoo's Nest became so famous that it was adapted to become a legendary addition to theater and film as well. Dale Wasserman made the novel into a two-act Broadway play (1974) starring Kirk Douglas, and a 2001 Broadway revival starring Gary Sinise and Amy Morton won the Tony Award for Best Play Revival. In 1975, Milos Forman directed a successful film adaptation of the novel. The film, recently named as one of the twenty greatest films by the American Film Institute, featured Jack Nicholson as R.P. McMurphy and Louise Fletcher as Nurse Ratched. The film also won the Academy Award for Best Picture and gained awards for Nicholson, Fletcher, and Forman. It remains one of only three films to have swept the top five categories at the Oscars.

Kesey originally was involved at the creative and production levels of the film, but he left two weeks into filming because he disagreed about dropping Chief Bromden's narration, because he objected to the casting of Jack Nicholson in the lead role (he wanted Gene Hackman), and because of a dispute over the $20,000 he was owed for the film rights. Kesey later would claim he never saw the film. Even so, his wife has said he generally supported the film and was pleased that it had been made.

Character List

Randall Patrick McMurphy

An imposing, red-headed Irishman, R.P. McMurphy enters the institution with a history of hostility, disobedience, and a recent conviction for statutory rape. Still, it is obvious from the start that he is a sane man who simply chose to accept institutionalization rather than live on a "work farm" as part of the judge's sentence. McMurphy is charismatic, sexual, and boisterous to the extreme--a "gambling fool" who looks out primarily for his own self-interest and matches wits with Nurse Ratched in the book's primary conflict. He also seems to care deeply about his fellow inmates, often putting justice and their well-being over his own desires to escape the institution--which inevitably costs him his sanity. McMurphy represents freedom and self-determination versus societal repression--a battle McMurphy ultimately loses in order to pave the way for the rest of the patients to see the light. In many ways, he becomes a sacrificial lamb for the sake of enlightenment and awakening, both within the novel and for readers. McMurphy's character is remembered as a martyr who inspires real-world social change.

Nurse Ratched

A middle-aged nurse who controls the institution where McMurphy is sentenced. Nurse Ratched (also known as Big Nurse) is stern, controlling, and determined to quash all resistance to her authority. Nurse Ratched believes in order above all, institutionalizing a systematized reduction of humans to robotic function, with an obliteration of all individual characteristics that might ultimately lead to rebellion. She is, in many ways, a metaphor for all forms of repression, particularly sexual repression. She seems to be ashamed of her own sexuality, consistently buttoned up in her white nurse's outfit, but she cannot hide her large breasts, her one incongruous physical trait. As a metaphor, then, it is only appropriate that her final comeuppance involves McMurphy (symbolizing freedom) tearing open her uniform and unleashing her breasts and body. As punishment, Ratched has McMurphy lobotomized. In that battle, authoritarianism, repression, and conservative sexuality win, but readers are led to fight against what Ratched represents.

Chief Bromden

A tall, half-Indian patient in the ward, Chief Bromden has been in the institution the longest. Although other inmates think that he is deaf and mute, Chief Bromden instead chooses not to speak, at first because others ignored him and then out of fear of Nurse Ratched. Chief Bromden is the narrator of the novel. With the help of McMurphy, he begins to speak once more and reasserts himself against Nurse Ratched and her workers. Ultimately, he breaks free of the Nurse and the hospital, killing the lobotimized McMurphy in order to prevent him from suffering further indignity, and finding his way back into society away from the repressive manipulation and tyrannical authority of the institution.

Billy Bibbit

A thirty-one-year-old patient in the institution, Billy Bibbit still appears very young, partly because of his persistent stutter. Bibbit is dominated and terrorized by his mother, who has intimidated him into behaving younger than his years and has instilled in him a strong sense of guilt. This guilt causes him to commit suicide after Nurse Ratched finds him with a prostitute and threatens to tell his mother.

Dale Harding

The president of the patients' council and a college graduate, Harding is likely the most educated patient in the institution. He explains many of the workings of the ward to McMurphy. Kesey indicates that Harding may be a closeted homosexual. Harding certainly is dominated by his boisterous wife, who intimidates him with her sexuality and his sexual inadequacy.

Bancini

A fifty-year-old resident in the institution, Bancini has been a "Chronic" since his birth, for his brain was damaged during childbirth. He had one moment of lucidity, when he claimed he was "tired" of life and had been dead since birth, but after being punished for this by Nurse Ratched, he succumbed to silence and the occasional whimpers of exhaustion.

Charles Cheswick

One of the patients on the ward, he is one of the first patients to support McMurphy, but he is taken to the Disturbed Ward, presumably for shock treatment, when he starts to protest the ward policies. Cheswick later dies in the swimming pool when he gets his fingers caught in the grate, an action that is possibly suicidal.

Ellis

Although formerly an "Acute," Ellis became a "Chronic" at the institution after receiving electroshock treatment.

Miss Flinn

One of the nurses in the ward, she talks with Nurse Ratched about McMurphy's possible motivation for wanting to disrupt the ward.

Frederickson

One of the patients on the ward, Frederickson takes the seizure medication that Sefelt refuses.

Geever

Geever is one of the black boys who works for Nurse Ratched and becomes her henchman in the management of the ward. Bromden makes the observation that these black boys are filled with hatred and thus enjoy punishing the inmates at Ratched's will.

Vera Harding

The wife of Dale Harding, Vera visits her husband at the institution and promptly gets into an argument with him. She is a physically imposing woman who uses her sexuality to intimidate her husband and who plays on his sexual insecurities.

Martini

One of the patients on the ward, Martini hallucinates that he sees objects on the board when the men play Monopoly. Despite his disruptions, McMurphy includes him in the games.

Colonel Matterson

The oldest Chronic in the ward, Colonel Matterson is a World War veteran who can now only utter incoherent phrases such as "the flag is America."

Nurse Pilbow

Nurse Pilbow is one of Ratched's nurses, a Catholic woman with a prominent birthmark that she attempts to wash away. She is intensely affected by feelings of guilt over her job and her sexuality.

Public Relation

A fat bureaucrat who often visits the ward, Public Relation attempts to frame the ward as a wonderful place to stay run with great generosity by Nurse Ratched.

Rawler

Rawler commits suicide one night, cutting off his testicles (suggesting that the ward leads patients to emasculate themselves).

Ruckly

A former Acute patient, Ruckly became a Chronic after electroshock treatment and now can only say over and over "fffffuck da wife."

Sandy Gilfilliam

One of the Portland prostitutes who was to accompany McMurphy and the men on the fishing trip, Sandy does not attend because she got married. Later, however, she divorces her husband and visits the institution with Candy, a fellow prostitute.

Scanlon

Scanlon is one of the Acute patients on the ward, the only patient who is involuntarily committed besides McMurphy.

Sefelt

Sefelt is an epileptic who refuses to take his seizure medicine because it destroys his gums. He tends to give his medication to Frederickson, who takes double doses in his stead. Sefelt, who has a legitimate medical condition, is often ignored by the staff, who seem more interested in dominating the rebellious patients.

George Sorenson

An old Swede nicknamed "Rub-a-Dub George" because of his obsession for cleanliness. A patient on the ward, George is a former fishing boat captain whom McMurphy cajoles into leading the fishing expedition. McMurphy later defends him when the black boys harass him during a humiliating cleansing, leading to the riot which prompts Ratched to send McMurphy and Bromden to "Disturbed."

Dr. Spivey

The main doctor on the ward, Dr. Spivey is easily manipulated by both Nurse Ratched and R.P. McMurphy, who in turn use him as a pawn. McMurphy uses him as his institutional defense on the ward, convincing him to open the tub room and to chaperone the patients on the fishing trip. Nurse Ratched, meanwhile, uses him to champion her authoritarian policies to discipline rebellious inmates.

Candy Starr

Candy Starr, a prostitute from Portland, chaperones McMurphy and the other patients on the fishing trip. McMurphy later plans a visit for Candy to the ward so that she may have sex with Billy Bibbit, with whom she became close during the fishing trip.

Mr. Taber

One of the patients on the ward, Mr. Taber complains to Nurse Ratched that he does not know what is in his medicine. Nurse Ratched claims that he was once a manipulator, like McMurphy, and she eventually made him quiescent through her tyrannical punishments.

Tee Ah Millatoona

Chief Bromden's father, also known as The Pine That Stands Tallest on the Mountain. An Indian chief, he married a Caucasian woman named Bromden and took her last name, but she ultimately drove him to alcoholism. He becomes a metaphor for the results of repression, obliteration, and in general the encroachment of authority on individualism.

Mr. Turkle

The night watchman on the ward. McMurphy bribes Mr. Turkle to allow Candy Starr into the ward.

Warren

Warren is one of the black boys who work for Nurse Ratched. Like Geever, he is one of her henchmen. He takes glee in torturing the inmates when she commands it.

Washington

Washington, like Geever and Warren, is one of the black boys who works for Nurse Ratched and follows her orders when commanded to round up and discipline one of the disobedient inmates.

Major Themes

Sexual Repression vs. Sexual Freedom

One of the prevailing motifs of Kesey's novel involves the metaphorical contrast between clamped-down sexual mores and freewheeling, instinctive, "natural" sexual freedom. The conflict is represented by the war between McMurphy and Nurse Ratched. The "Big Nurse" represents a frigid, controlled sexuality, an attempt to button up natural instincts and resist impulse through conscious order. She cannot, however, disguise her huge breasts, which show through her uniform no matter how much she covers up. McMurphy, the symbol of total sexual abandon, ultimately tears the Nurse's clothes from her body to "unleash" her breasts in a final climax of the battle. McMurphy himself is almost animalistic in his sexuality, which is a main reason he has been institutionalized by a repressive society. He is considered dangerous and hostile because he acts on his urges. His primary crime is statutory rape, an offense he defends by arguing that the young girl pressed him to have sex rather than the other way around. At the end of the novel, though McMurphy frees nearly all the main characters sexually--bringing a prostitute for fellow inmates, encouraging the men to rediscover the emasculated souls they've surrendered to Nurse Ratched--he must pay for his free sexuality by losing a part of his brain. Kesey suggests that fully unfettered sexuality is too dangerous for modern society to tolerate.

Independence vs. Acquiescence

Throughout the novel, we consistently root for the inmates to find freedom, either through a mass escape or by overthrowing the regime and winning a new order in the institution. This is all subverted, however, when McMurphy discovers that he and Scanlon are the only two involuntarily committed inmates. The rest of the inmates are there by choice. They would rather be quiescent followers, surrendering themselves to institutional oppression, than independent in a society where they do not quite fit and may not be able to function. McMurphy sees emasculation as the prime reason for the choice to stay. The Nurse has found a way to mentally castrate each and every one of the inmates--including Rawlins, who commits suicide by physical emasculation. McMurphy may perceive that the best way to free the other men is to expose Nurse Ratched as flesh and blood rather than an inevitable oppressor--someone with her own flaws and pains. McMurphy attempts to work within the Nurse's system, trying to outmanipulate and outfox her with his various schemes. But ultimately, the only way to change the acquiescence of his fellow inmates is to lead by example. He feels presure to acquiesce and avoid pain, but he choose to follow his independent spirit, which explodes in brute force when he rips the Nurse's clothes open. This act prevents the rest of the inmates from ever seeing her as merely the robotic hand of authority. She has a body now, and they can no longer follow her blindly, understanding that she is just as mortal as they are. They are likely to continue choosing the institution to the outside world, but they will remain with a greater degree of independence than before.

Self-Interest vs. Altruism

McMurphy's character is worth considering in comparing the drives for altruism and self-interest. When McMurphy enters the hospital, he has the goal of causing chaos in order to disrupt Nurse Ratched's carefully designed schemes, which quash the inmates' spirits. At first it seems that he does so primarily for amusement, or in order to establish himself as Top Dog and ensure that he has the power in the ward. He also consistently fleeces the other inmates in gambling games. Over time, however, we suspect that money, power, and amusement are not—or are no longer—his primary motivation for taking on Ratched. He develops a sincere desire to resuscitate these fallen, empty, drained souls. In one of the most significant moments of the novel, when he is frustrated that the men are not trying to get out, he throws all their money back at them, in a demonstration that he cares more about them than self-interest alone would dictate. Once McMurphy realizes that he might never get out, being involuntarily committed subject to Ratched's will, he for a while follows his self-interest. But this is temporary, for he ultimately sacrifices himself in order to allow the inmates to see their chance for escape from the ward in both body and soul.

Mind vs. Matter

Kesey's novel elucidates some ways that people imprison themselves psychosomatically, using the mind to trap the body. In the case of Chief Bromden, for instance, the Indian has convinced others—maybe even himself—that he is deaf and dumb. This chosen handicap dictates the conditions of even the most mundane moments of his life. Meanwhile, for the rest of the inmates, in group therapy sessions Nurse Ratched uses the power of suggestion to expose their deepest insecurities. We see over and over that belief in a particular ailment seems to induce it. Specifically, in the case of electroshock therapy (EST), given to disturbed patients whenever they misbehave, most of them succumb and find themselves changed negatively by the experience. Chief Bromden, in particular, says that fighting EST was not an option: the fog simply envelops you and warps your brain. But McMurphy teaches him that fighting EST requires willpower, and through focus of mind it can be resisted like much else. Again and again, McMurphy uses his strength to fight the effect of EST, allowing Bromden to follow him and finally escape. There are natural limits—namely, nature itself—to the use of mind over matter. Some people have genuine medical conditions. Ratched herself cannot wish away her large bosom. As for McMurphy, he cannot withstand Ratched's final tool of punishment, the actual removal of part of his brain.

Fear vs. Experience

The inmates tend to be prisoners of their own fear. Kesey suggests that modern society, figured by Nurse Ratched's institution, preys on fear, that authoritarian, repressive regimes, whether in the government, the home, or the workplace, rely on fear to control individuals. Ratched's methods of manipulation include using public embarrassment to make the inmates turn on each other, then the power of suggestion to make the inmates afraid of her potential to expose each one of their unique flaws to the group. She uses a carrot-and-stick approach to make the inmates afraid of physical punishment for the slightest disobedience. What McMurphy finds upon entering the ward is a group of sniveling, whipped animals who have lost the sense of their own capacity for learning from everyday experience. They have given up sex, alcohol, and even living voluntarily because of their fear of indulging in everyday life. Whatever fear of life brought most of them into the institution in the first place has been magnified many times by Ratched's regime, and McMurphy takes up the challenge of helping the others again want to experience more out of life.

Origins of Violence

Many critics have mistakenly cried racism against Kesey in the novel's depiction of the three black boys who serve Nurse Ratched. They certainly are portrayed as dumb, sniveling brutes who follow the Nurse's orders as perverse henchmen. They are intent on destruction. Why did Kesey choose to make these characters black? Kesey's choice is not racist but is a critique of racism in society or at least racism in Ratched's mind. This is because the novel provides a very clear etiology for each of these boys early in the novel. The Nurse carefully sorts through potential boys for the job, looking for the ones who have the most hate within them, those who have learned to internalize their rage so that they have every reason to be completely obedient to her will and to act brutally when they get the chance. Nurse Ratched has chosen boys who already express the internalized anger she feels, the fury and pain she has repressed under the facade of calm, serene order. If the boys who fit the bill are black, it is because in a racist society they already have experienced (more than others) the hurt in their lives that has made them so angry, and if anyone is racist in this regard, it is Ratched for thinking the black boys are most likely to be the kind of boys she wants. If one's environment is largely to blame for a person becoming angry and violent, it is worth examining the causes of anger and violence in other characters from the same perspective.

Group Mentality vs. Individualism

Perhaps Nurse Ratched's most sinister tool is preying on the group mentality of the inmates to instill fear and self-loathing. She makes it very clear that the inmates are not allowed to be on their own; they must form groups of eight in order to request access to even the most mundane activity. There is method to this seeming draconian order. The Nurse knows that as long as the men can reflect, mirror, and expose each other's pain, they will have enough to occupy themselves with rather than rebelling against her. Only in the solitude of one's own room can one of them look inside and develop the strength of will and character to begin questioning her authority. Such questioning of the hospital, its leadership, the role of the hospital in their convalescence, or broadly questioning authority or society is a mark of individualism that Nurse Ratched will not allow. In a group of disturbed people, the group identity is going nowhere, and that is the way she wants it. She controls the inmates by controlling the questions asked, and as long as she prevents them from being alone for very long, she knows that she will have the upper hand.

Glossary of Terms

Acutes

The inmates who have treatable conditions. The hospital expects that they someday will be able to return to functioning in society. They are generally the most lucid of the inmates and the ones who can take care of themselves. The worst possible punishment is for an Acute to be turned over to the Chronic ward, such as if the nurse notices a consistent thread of disobedience that suggests the patient is not going to recover--or if a vindictive nurse just wants it to seem that way.

chabobs

One of McMurphy's more lewd epithets referring to breasts, particularly Nurse Ratched's large ones.

Chronics

Those whose mental impairments are such that they have no hope to return to functioning in society. They operate as their own dysfunctional cabal. They essentially have surrendered their lives to the hospital.

Combine

One of Chief Bromden's hallucinations, a systematized, robotic, control mechanism that demands human obedience. He consistently imagines that he hears the machine sounds of the Combine in the silence of the hospital.

convalescents

Green uniforms the inmates are asked to wear during their stay at the hospital--another way of eliminating individualism on the ward.

Dilantin

An anti-seizure drug. Sefel refuses to take it even though he is an epileptic because he is afraid it makes his hair fall out and gums go black.

Disturbed

The "Disturbed" wing of the hospital is the much-feared floor where the most disobedient inmates are sent to receive electroshock therapy or other physical punishments for their disobedience. Inmates often come down from Disturbed quite changed, quiescent because of their experiences. The Nurse has the power to send someone up to Disturbed. She sends both Chief Bromden and McMurphy up after they beat up her henchmen boys during a shower incident.

electroshock therapy

EST, a form of therapy whereby electrodes are attached to the head and a force of electrical current is sent into the brain. The idea is to cause a virtual "reset" of the brain waves. After doctors noticed that EST tamed wild cattle, they used it for many years to tame the most inscrutable institutionalized patients, only to abandon the so-called treatment in later years after the numerous and palpable negative side effects were studied and made public.

Shock Shop

The Shock Shop in Building One is where the most disturbed patients are sent for electroshock therapy to punish them for disobedience.

Short Summary

One Flew Over the Cuckoo's Nest takes place in a mental institution in the Pacific Northwest. The narrator of the novel is Chief Bromden, also known as Chief Broom, a catatonic half-Indian man whom all of the inmates and staff assume is deaf and dumb. Bromden often suffers from hallucinations during which he feels the room filling with a dense, overwhelming fog generated by a huge mechanized matrix called The Combine which controls everyone in its grasp. The institution is dominated by Nurse Ratched (Big Nurse), a cold, precise woman with calculated gestures and a calm, mechanical manner. When the story begins, a new patient, Randall Patrick McMurphy, arrives at the ward. He is a self-professed "gambling fool" who has just come from a work farm at Pendleton as part of his sentence for statutory rape. He clearly is completely sane and lucid, at the hospital only to avoid the work detail. Others on the ward include Dale Harding, the president of the patient's council, and Billy Bibbit, a thirty-year-old who stutters and appears very young. Ratched immediately pegs McMurphy as a manipulator.

During the first therapy meeting, Nurse Ratched begins examining Harding's difficulties with his wife. McMurphy takes the opportunity to explain his arrest for statutory rape, suggesting that the girl was of legal age and certainly more than consenting. Dr. Spivey, the main doctor for the ward, questions whether McMurphy is now feigning insanity to get out of doing hard labor at the work farm. Afterward, McMurphy confronts Harding about the way the inmates defer to Ratched so readily. He suggests it is a "pecking-party" in which the patients are to turn on each other. Harding admits that all of the patients and even Dr. Spivey are afraid of the Big Nurse. He adds that the patients are rabbits who cannot adjust to their rabbithood and need Big Nurse to show them their place. McMurphy bets him that he can get Nurse Ratched to crack within a week.

McMurphy awakens early the next morning to take a shower. He complains to one of the black boys who serve as Nurse Ratched's henchmen that the patients are only allowed to brush their teeth at certain times. When Ratched arrives, McMurphy stands in front of her in a towel, claiming that his clothes have been taken. He threatens to drop his towel (though he has shorts on). Ratched screams to one of the boys to get McMurphy some new clothes.

McMurphy then complains to Ratched about the loud music that constantly plays on the ward, but she refuses to turn it down. He suggests opening the tub room as a game room, but she refuses. At the next group meeting, Dr. Spivey mentions casually that he talked to McMurphy about opening up the tub room as a game room and thinks that it is a great idea. The other inmates ratify the plan while Nurse Ratched's hands begin to shake—her first significant sign of weakness.

McMurphy next pushes for a schedule change so the patients can watch the World Series during the day and do their work at night. He attempts to motivate the patients to push for the schedule change, but he becomes angry at them when they act too "chicken-shit" and refuse to oppose Ratched. Billy Bibbit tells McMurphy that nothing he can do will be of any use in the long run, but McMurphy boasts that he will break out of the institution by lifting up the control panel in the tub room and throwing it through the window.

The patients gradually grow more assertive in their opposition to the boys and to Ratched. At another group meeting, after Billy discusses his stutter and having proposed to a woman his mother disliked, McMurphy brings up the World Series again. Ratched finally allows a vote. All twenty Acute patients vote for his idea, but Ratched declares it a defeat, for none of the Chronics have had the ability to vote. McMurphy finally motivates Chief Bromden to vote for him, but Ratched says it is too late and the vote is over. As a protest, McMurphy refuses to work and sits down in front of the television while the World Series is on. The other patients join him in this mutiny.

During a staff meeting, the doctors discuss McMurphy with Ratched. They believe that he is no ordinary man and might be dangerous. Ratched, however, claims that McMurphy is not an extraordinary man and is subject to all the fears and timidity of the other men. She is confident that she can break McMurphy, for he is committed to the hospital and they are in control, able to decide when he will be released.

McMurphy continues to behave aggressively, but Ratched does not respond. The other patients revisit longstanding gripes against her, such as the rationing of cigarettes and the tight control over their schedules. When the men make their weekly trip to the pool, McMurphy learns that he will only be released after Nurse Ratched and the doctors decide he is ready. At the next group meeting, Cheswick complains about the rationing of cigarettes, and two of the boys are required to drag him away to the Disturbed Ward. He returns, presumably after having undergone shock treatment. Soon after, Cheswick drowns when he gets his fingers stuck in the grate at the bottom of the pool.

Nurse Ratched reassumes her control over the ward after McMurphy gives up his struggle against her, knowing that she controls whether or not he leaves. On the ward's trip to the library, Harding introduces McMurphy to his visiting wife, Vera. Harding and Vera are rude to one another, and she implies that he is a closeted homosexual, then suddenly leaves. Harding asks McMurphy his opinion, and McMurphy snaps that he will not say how awful Vera is, even if that is what Harding wants to hear. McMurphy says he has his own worries and should not have to deal with others' problems.

While getting chest X-rays for TB in another part of the hospital, McMurphy learns about the Shock Shop, where patients get electroshock therapy, and he learns about lobotomies, partial brain removal designed to tame the wildest patients. He confronts Harding and the other patients about why they never told him directly that Nurse Ratched controls whether or not he leaves. They claim to have forgotten he was involuntarily committed, for with rare exceptions, all of the others entered the hospital voluntarily. McMurphy cannot conceive that these men would choose to live in the hospital, but Billy tells him that they are too weak to leave.

Nurse Ratched closes the tub room that the patients had been using for several weeks, on the ground that the men did not apologize for their behavior during the World Series protest. McMurphy responds by punching the glass at the Nurses' Station. Ratched does little to retaliate because she knows she can prolong the fight. McMurphy requests an Accompanied Pass to go deep-sea fishing and tries to recruit patients to go with him. In response, Ratched posts newspaper clippings about the dangers of boating, which frighten several patients.

McMurphy realizes that Chief Bromden is neither deaf nor dumb. One night McMurphy offers Bromden a pack of chewing gum and gets him to speak about his family. McMurphy suggests that Bromden pick up the control panel in the tub room and throw it through the window so that he can escape. McMurphy signs up Bromden for the fishing trip.

On the day of the trip, Nurse Ratched tries to derail it, for only one of the chaperones (a prostitute named Candy Starr) has arrived instead of two. Dr. Spivey, however, acts as the second chaperone. When they stop for gas on the way to the docks, the gas-station attendant asks if they are patients from the asylum. Dr. Spivey claims that they are merely a work crew, but McMurphy boldly brags that they are criminally insane. At the docks, a couple of men yell disparaging comments about Candy and the patients. McMurphy has trouble securing the boat because they lack a waiver, but he takes the boat without a captain. After a day of fishing, the men return rejuvenated, and the men on the docks no longer mock them.

Nurse Ratched makes her next move against McMurphy by posting the patients' financial statements, which show that McMurphy has made a profit against the other patients since he arrived. She suggests in a meeting that McMurphy is trying to manipulate them. When the men confront McMurphy about this, he admits that he is no saint, but he has been perfectly honest about his intentions. He arranges for Candy to visit the institution for a visit with Billy Bibbit. During a cautionary cleansing that Nurse Ratched orders, several of the black boys harass one of the patients, George Sorenson. McMurphy defends him and gets in a fight with them. Chief Bromden joins in when the black boys gang up on McMurphy, and both men are taken away to the Disturbed Ward.

Down at the Disturbed Ward, a nurse treats McMurphy's and Bromden's wounds and tells them that not every ward is run as autocratically as Nurse Ratched's. The nurse adds that she wishes she could keep patients away from her ward. Ratched gives McMurphy and Bromden a chance to apologize before administering shock treatment. McMurphy refuses. They administer shock treatment to him several times in one week, even though Bromden tries to talk him into complying. McMurphy claims that the electroshock therapy energizes him. When Bromden returns to the ward, Harding congratulates him and tells the Chief that he has heard rumors that McMurphy is not responding at all to the EST. Ratched brings McMurphy back to the ward after she learns that his absence and resistance have led to his becoming an inspirational "legend."

Harding and the other patients decide to engineer McMurphy's escape when Candy arrives on a Saturday night for her meeting with Billy. They bribe Mr. Turkle, the night watchman, with liquor and an offer of sex with Candy, and the other patients have a party that night. McMurphy delays leaving until early in the morning, however, and falls asleep. The black boys find him the next morning.

When Nurse Ratched arrives, she gathers the patients together in one room to take roll. She realizes that Billy Bibbit is missing. She finds him in the Seclusion Room with Candy. She chastises him for having sex with such a cheap woman, then tells him that she will tell his mother. Billy begins to stutter at this, but she takes him into the doctor's office to calm down. When the doctor arrives, he finds that Billy has cut his throat and killed himself. Ratched blames McMurphy for Billy's suicide, and he responds by trying to strangle her. Although the black boys pull McMurphy off of her before he can kill her, he rips her uniform, exposing her breasts.

Nurse Ratched takes time off to recuperate, and when she returns, she cannot speak. Many of the patients check out of the hospital. Weeks later, McMurphy returns to the ward, now comatose after having a forced lobotomy. Chief Bromden smothers McMurphy with a pillow in order to put him out of his misery, then throws the control panel in the tub room through the window and escapes the institution, fulfilling McMurphy's escape plan for himself.

Summary and Analysis of Part One, Chapters 1-5

Chapter One

One Flew Over the Cuckoo's Nest is narrated by Chief Bromden (also known as Chief Broom), a mute Indian who ritually mops the mental institution where he is confined. The black boys in white suits who work in the ward mock Chief Broom, assuming that he is deaf and dumb and cannot hear them. Chief Broom never speaks, but we can hear his thoughts.

Nurse Ratched (also known as Big Nurse) enters, her lips and her fingernails both an odd orange. She carries a woven wicker bag filled with pills, needles, wire, and forceps. She moves with precise, automatic gestures, her face at once determined and calculated, but she cannot seem to hide her large breasts, which seem incongruous with the rest of her body and disposition. Ruthless and mechanical, she orders the black boys to shave Chief Bromden, who quickly hides in terror. While hiding, he thinks about his father and growing up on the banks of the Columbia River. Soon, one of the boys finds him, and they start to shave him. Terrified, the Chief hallucinates that an Air Raid has begun in the ward and that a thick fog begins to overwhelm him.

Chapter Two

When the fog clears, Bromden realizes he is not in the Shock Shop, where patients are given electroshock treatment, so he relaxes. At that moment, an escort brings in another patient for admission. Nurse Ratched quickly orders that he receive a shower. The patient, a red-haired Irishman named Randall Patrick McMurphy, quickly retorts that every place he goes requires a shower—the courthouse, the jail—and he is already as clean as clean can be. He introduces his tall, strapping self to the ward as a "gambling fool" and takes out his pack of cards. McMurphy has arrived from a work farm named Pendleton, and he is wearing the shirt and pants of his farm uniform—and a leather jacket. McMurphy brags that he is a psychopath, but he clearly gives the impression that he is quite lucid.

Chapter Three

The younger patients are known as Acutes because the doctors in the ward see them as possessing acute or temporary conditions, not chronic mental illness. Therefore they have been deemed capable of being treated and ultimately turned back to society, having become able to function there. Billy Bibbit, one of the Acutes, tries to roll a cigarette, while Martini, another Acute, ambles around the ward. The Acutes take up half of the ward, and the other half is filled with the Chronics, who are in the hospital for good. Some of these include the "Walkers," like Chief Broom, who retain their physical capabilities, while others are "Vegetables," essentially comatose. A number of the Chronics used to be Acutes until they began receiving large doses of electroshock therapy (EST). Ruckly and Ellis, for instance, were Acutes who were essentially lobotomized by intense EST. Ruckly now can only say "ffffuck da wife" over and over in a low, creepy tone. Colonel Matterson is the oldest Chronic, a World War I veteran, and Chief Bromden has been in the ward the longest.

McMurphy arrives, circling the Acutes to ask which one is "bull goose loony," the craziest one to reckon with. In other words, he is asking who is really in charge. Billy Bibbit, a young man who stutters, introduces McMurphy to Harding, the president of the patients' council. Harding is a flat, nervous man and a college graduate. McMurphy tells Harding that there is not room for two bull goose loonies, so Harding will have to step aside. Harding and McMurphy compete to show their lunacy, both claiming they voted for Eisenhower. Harding finally defers to him, and McMurphy introduces himself to everybody, even the Chronics. He finally centers his attention on Chief Bromden. Harding tells McMurphy that Bromden is only half Indian and is deaf and dumb.

Nurse Ratched summons McMurphy and tells him that he must take his admission shower, for everybody must follow the rules. He answers that this what everyone tells him every time they figure he is about to do the opposite.

Chapter Four

Nurse Ratched prepares hypodermic needles as a nurse asks her opinion of McMurphy. Ratched claims McMurphy is a "manipulator" who will use everyone and everything to his own ends. She claims that sometimes a manipulator's end is to disrup the ward. The nurse, Miss Flinn, asks what the motive would be, but Nurse Ratched reminds her that this is an insane asylum.

Chief Bromden notes how Ratched elicits complete control of the staff of the ward, which he now officially names the Combine. Even the doctors are obedient to her, and she has managed to organize a group of henchmen, the sadistic black boys. Most of all, Nurse Ratched is a believer in routine. Each morning she dispenses medications and sets about a carefully controlled scheme of actions. On this day, however, Mr. Taber demands to know what is in his medication, and Nurse Ratched refuses to say. Instead, she remarks coldly that there are means of taking the medicine other than orally. The black boys take him away and inject him.

Chapter Five

Nurse Ratched calls a ward meeting. She interrupts Pete Bancini, who complains that he is tired, and tells the black boys to quiet him. Nobody will look at Ratched except for McMurphy, who still has his cap and deck of cards. She starts the meeting by bringing up Harding's marital problems. She reiterates how Harding is concerned about his well-endowed young wife and the attention she receives, as well as his own feelings of inferiority. She asks for comments, and McMurphy raises his hand.

McMurphy ignores the question and introduces himself as a Korean War veteran dishonorably discharged for insubordination and subsequently convicted of statutory rape. McMurphy argues with Dr. Spivey about who was the aggressor in that case, he or the young girl. Spivey questions whether McMurphy is merely a sane man feigning psychosis to escape the drudgery of farm work. Ratched tells McMurphy the theory of the Therapeutic Community: a person must learn to get along in a group before he will be able to function in society. Bancini, a fifty-year-old man who has been a Chronic all his life (his brain was damaged during childbirth), interrupts again to say that he is tired. Ratched orders the boys to take him for treatment after he starts ranting and raving.

After the meeting, McMurphy asks if the meeting procedure is always such a "pecking party," where all the inmates descend on each other. Harding defends Nurse Ratched and claims that she is a strict middle-aged lady, but no monster. McMurphy replies that she has him by the balls. Harding claims that she is a "veritable angel of mercy" who is "unselfish as the wind"—but Harding finally relents and admits that McMurphy is right, only no one has actually said so before. Harding notes that Dr. Spivey, just like the patients, is afraid of Nurse Ratched. Harding compares the patients to rabbits who cannot adjust to their rabbithood, so they need a strong wolf like Nurse Ratched to teach them their places.

McMurphy says to the men that deep down, they are all lucid and can return to functioning society. Harding now relates the tools that Ratched uses to gain submission from the patients, including domination and even electroshock therapy (EST). McMurphy bets the patients that he can get Nurse Ratched to "crack" or show some vulnerability within a week.

Analysis

In the first chapter, Kesey sets up the hierarchy, geography, and structures of the mental institution which serves as the novel's setting. The book's authority figure, the villain, is clearly Nurse Ratched, also known as Big Nurse, a woman whose characteristics are described as almost inhuman. Kesey makes her essentially a mechanized robot, completely devoted to order, precision, and control. She is an emblem of bureaucracy and authority, unable to feel compassion or recognize men as individuals. Instead, she believes simply in domination and the stamping out of individual characteristics in subjugation to group order. Still, even in this first chapter, there are indications that behind this inhuman facade lies a mortal instability. She seems ready to snap at the black boys at any moment and unleash her animalistic rage, barely suppressed. Besides, her breasts cannot be disguised, revealing that she is incapable of fully hiding her essential humanity.

The black boys at the institution, meanwhile, serve Nurse Ratched out of fear, though they are good for the job of serving her because their most prominent characteristic is their complete hatred for everyone around them. They are sadistic. Having them around permits Ratched to stay above the fray while the boys become her henchmen, externalizing her repressed anger. For her and for the reader, the boys serve as metaphors for the Nurse's deeply suppressed rage.

Although Chief Bromden is the story's narrator, at this point he cannot be trusted fully since his reliability is in question. For one thing, he is prone to hallucinations, most of which involve the Combine, a matrix which allows civil wars to erupt within the ward at the whim of a huge bureaucratic, unnamed "machine" government. The fog that descends is a metaphor for Bromden's lack of mental clarity, thickening whenever he becomes less stable, receding as he gains confidence. It also is significant that Bromden chooses to remain silent, representing the quiescent persons of society who relinquish their own voices when confronted with authority.

In the second chapter, we meet the protagonist, Randall Patrick McMurphy, who will lock horns with the villain, Nurse Ratched. McMurphy is exuberant, vital, vulgar—everything in his personality suggests a great torrent of energy and a great lack of control. Whereas Nurse Ratched represents bureaucracy and control, McMurphy represents the counterculture, for he is liberated, open, in touch with his true self. McMurphy might brag about being a psychopath, but it is easy to discern the ruse, for he is boisterous, entertaining, quick with words, and oddly gentle in his mannerisms. He clings to the idea that he belongs at the ward, but we already sense that he is the only lucid patient in the ward. We will rely on him to illuminate the true sanity and humanness of others. Even so, he is there for a reason. It is only because of statutory rape and avoiding the work farm, or is there a real problem with his open flouting of authority? Does his independence go too far in a repressive society that is not ready for the likes of a countercultural free spirit?

In Chapter Three, having described the support staff of the hospital, Chief Bromden turns to the patients who inhabit the institution. Most of the patients are Acutes, meaning that they have the possibility of rehabilitation and release, but Bromden makes the important point that they also have the possibility of worsening at the hands of Nurse Ratched and ultimately becoming Chronics like Ruckly and Ellis. Billy Bibbit and Harding stand out as important characters, and both will play major roles in the novel. Harding is most significant now because of his role as the leader of the patients. He leads by virtue of his education, but McMurphy already begins to usurp his power through his charisma and ebullience.

The lines of conflict between McMurphy and Nurse Ratched are already forming. She represents rules and order, while McMurphy represents anarchy, sexual freedom, and disobedience. They sense that this is going to be the root of their conflicts. McMurphy also is a threat to the order of the ward because of his showmanship. He grasps for attention, behaving like a politician on a campaign stop in order to be Top Dog. This choice to gain social approval rather than to be thoroughly an individualist will cause McMurphy to be an easy target for those in the institution, particularly Nurse Ratched. Such a choice also is an early sign that McMurphy will not simply be solipsistic on the ward and will take concern for the other men.

In Chapter Four, Nurse Ratched develops further as an unfeeling automaton dedicated to the service of bureaucracy. She is dispassionate and overly analytical, concerned primarily with the smooth functioning of the ward over any personal concerns. Her main insecurity involves the balance of power in the asylum. McMurphy is a threat to Nurse Ratched because he proves dangerous to the autocratic control she exerts over the others. The black boys, the nurses, and even the doctors are completely submissive to Nurse Ratched's authority, but McMurphy is not yet playing along. It is notable that her control is based as much on intimidation and hatred as efficiency, as demonstrated in this chapter by her threat against Mr. Taber.

Also in this chapter, Chief Bromden opens a critique of the mental institution into a larger societal critique. The social criticism here is based on the idea that the institution, even though it is for the mentally ill, is a microcosm of the rest of society. The mental institution is meant to repair damage done to people's minds in various ways by religions, schools, and families, yet it operates in the same culture and under the same basic conditions as such organizations and thus suffers the same problems of control and conformity versus individual freedom.

The ward meetings in Chapter Five demonstrate the intimidation and domination techniques that Ratched uses to exert her control. The meeting begins with Nurse Ratched selecting a patient and humiliating him by describing his personal and psychological problems, then asking the other patients to comment on the problems she has described. Her purpose is to pit the patients against one another, thus fostering division among the patients so that they remain submissive to her as the true leader. McMurphy accurately describes this as a pecking party, for the patients are to attack each other as a distraction from the control which she is exerting over them.

The other patients, in particular Harding, realize Nurse Ratched's domination, but they blindly accept this problem as either necessary or insurmountable. Nurse Ratched even has control over the doctors and administrative staff of the hospital, so what could the patients do? Harding suggests that she is part of a matriarchy related to his problems with his wife and his sexual difficulties. Although they implicitly acknowledge Nurse Ratched's control, they do not resist because they have come to believe it is necessary for their convalescence and perhaps for their return to society. Since the inmates believe themselves to be weak, they accept the presence of an authority to control them, which is an important reason they have chosen to be in the asylum. In fact, most are capable of independent action, but they see no reason to resist. McMurphy remains the exception, alone resisting Nurse Ratched's control. This independence marks him as possibly sane, leading Dr. Spivey to suggest that McMurphy is feigning insanity in order to stay out of the work-farm. Spivey is likely right, for McMurphy is able to reason Harding into admitting openly that Ratched is the oppressor McMurphy says she is.

Summary and Analysis of Part One, Chapters 6-9

Chapter Six

Bromden says that Nurse Ratched can set the wall clock at whatever speed she chooses just by turning a dial in the door. She generally slows time down to keep the patients at her mercy. Meanwhile, the speakers on the ceiling are playing music loudly, so McMurphy complains to Harding, who explains that they hear music nearly all the time, but never the news because the news might not be therapeutic. McMurphy goes into the Nurses' Station to complain, and one of the nurses, Miss Pilbow, tells him to stay back, apparently because she is a Catholic and may have heard that McMurphy is a sex maniac. He merely picks up a watering can that the nurse dropped. Soon after, McMurphy realizes that Bromden is not deaf, for Bromden jumps whenever McMurphy claims that one of the boys is coming for him.

Chapter Seven

For the first time in a long while, Chief Bromden goes to sleep without taking the little red capsule, which normally makes him fall into a heavy slumber. That night, Chief Bromden dreams for the first time in a while. In the dream, he sees the workers lifting Blastic, one of the Vegetables, onto a hook and slicing him open with a scalpel. No blood comes out, only glass, rust, and ashes, the contents of a broken machine. Bromden thinks of waking up everyone, but he thinks that the workers would do the same to him. Mr. Turkle pulls Bromden out of the fog, telling him that he was having a bad dream.

Chapter Eight

The next morning, McMurphy is awake early, singing. Most of the people on the ward floor have not heard singing in years. Bromden wonders why the black boys allow such loud noise, but he soon realizes that McMurphy is different. He may be as vulnerable as the rest in the ward, but the Combine has not gotten to him. McMurphy asks for toothpaste to brush his teeth, but a boy tells him that it is ward policy to have the toothpaste locked up and only used at a certain time. McMurphy mocks the boy's question, "What would it be like if everybody was to brush their teeth whenever they felt like it?" Nurse Ratched arrives, and the boy tells her that Blastic died the night before and that McMurphy has been confrontational. Then she hears McMurphy singing. He steps out of the shower in a towel and stands in front of her. She tells him he cannot run around in a towel, and he prepares to drop it, telling her that someone stole his clothes. She chastises Mr. Washington, one of the boys, and orders him to get McMurphy a new set of clothes.

Chapter Nine

McMurphy clowns around during breakfast, embarrassing Billy Bibbit by claiming that Billy is known as "Billy Club" Bibbit of the famous fourteen inches. McMurphy bets the other patients that he can fling a dab of butter into the center of the face of the clock. He misses, but the butter slides down to the clock, hitting the face.

McMurphy complains to Nurse Ratched about the loud music in the hall, but she retorts that he is being selfish, for older men could not hear the radio at all if it were at a lower volume, and the music is all that they have. McMurphy suggests that patients be allowed to take their card games someplace else, such as the room where the tables are stored, but she replies that they do not have adequate personnel for two separate day rooms.

McMurphy has an interview with the doctor. During the daily meeting, the doctor tells the patients that he and McMurphy went to the same high school, and they reminisced about their school's carnivals. He suggests a similar carnival for the ward. The patients reluctantly take to this idea. Nurse Ratched tells the doctor that an idea like this should be discussed in a staff meeting first. Dr. Spivey also mentions that McMurphy was concerned that the older fellows could not hear the radio. Since the younger men have complained about the noise, McMurphy suggests opening a second day room as a game room—the plan that Nurse Ratched recently shot down. Dr. Spivey believes that there is sufficient staff to cover two rooms. When they return to the normal business of the meeting, Nurse Ratched's hands seem to shake. Chief Bromden thinks that this is a sign of her terrible weakness, though he realizes she has the Combine at her disposal to silence the opposition.

Analysis

In Chapter Six, Chief Bromden's suggestion that Nurse Ratched can control the clocks at the ward reveals his paranoia. At the same time, his suggestion provides a sense of the thoroughness with which Nurse Ratched has enacted her domination. Controlling time in this way seems entirely consistent with her controlling character.

Harding continues to serve the plot by providing exposition, explaining to McMurphy the routines and tenets of the ward, including the loud music.

This chapter also highlights the contrast between McMurphy and Nurse Ratched in terms of sexuality. In his confrontation with Nurse Pilbow, McMurphy represents a dangerous sexuality, the opposite of the passionless and repressed Nurse Ratched.

Chief Bromden's dream in Chapter Seven presents his fear that all the men in the ward are turning into mechanized vegetables, losing their capacity to feel, to live, and ultimately to rediscover their own souls. Rather than helping them, their stay at the hospital is slowly obliterating everything inside of them and replacing it with machine-like deadness. At the same time, the Chief still seems unreliable as a narrator in that he is apt to completely lose track of reality at the slightest trigger. He normally does not dream because of the pills that plunge him into heavy slumbers.

Now, however, with the opportunity to dream, his subconscious is unleashed, and while this nightmare is not so different from those of sane people, his reaction suggests that he is in another fog. Perhaps he senses that he has reached a critical point where he either must fight back to lucidity or surrender to the fate of Blastic. McMurphy will be pivotal in helping Chief Bromden choose to start recovering.

In Chapter Eight, McMurphy exposes some of the ward's inane policies. He realizes ways in which the ward impedes a person's ability to make rational decisions. Even deciding when to brush one's teeth is no longer a choice for the ward residents. The boy's response invokes, hilariously, the chaos that would ensue if people brushed their teeth willy-nilly. Such arguments are the irrational arguments of control for control's sake; all too often, an authority figure has no good reason for a rule and can only try to scare off the inquirer by invoking an impossible, extreme case.

Chief Bromden perceives that McMurphy is different from the other characters. Bromden's way of expressing this is to say that McMurphy has not been transformed by the Combine. McMurphy's antisocial history may play a large part in this assessment; he has not yet had the experience of drudge work and responsibility to subdue him. This puts him in substantial contrast to Harding, whose sense of responsibility plays a large role in his psychoses.

The confrontation between Nurse Ratched and McMurphy has clear sexual undertones. Indeed, one of the major themes of the novel involves the contrast between liberated and repressed sexuality. By appearing in front of Nurse Ratched wearing only a towel—and threatening to lose even that—McMurphy confronts her with the prospect of forbidden nakedness. In their final major confrontation, it will be Ratched whose nakedness is exposed against all propriety and at the hands of McMurphy. The fact that McMurphy is actually wearing boxer shorts reveals that he is playing a game with Ratched and figures correctly that she is vulnerable to his charms or at least to his threats of startling activity. Significantly, this is the first moment at which Nurse Ratched shows any strain or tension. McMurphy thus begins to find a place for a wedge and make Big Nurse crack, in line with the bet that he made with other patients.

Although One Flew Over the Cuckoo's Nest can be construed as a parable pitting the counterculture (McMurphy) against the establishment (Ratched), McMurphy is too complex to be set up merely as a metaphor. If McMurphy is a challenge to the establishment, he also attempts to work within it. Dr. Spivey has power in the ward that McMurphy hopes to redirect against Ratched and in favor of McMurphy's desires and the needs of the men. His request in Chapter Nine to have the music volume lowered is also an acknowledgment of Ratched's power, and the request is both rational and diplomatic. Similarly, his counterproposal to open the tub room as a game room for the patients also seems appropriate.

Nurse Ratched seems less complex. True to her controlling character, she is not interested in working with McMurphy to change anything. In rejecting his requests, she demonstrates her dominance over him and refuses to empower him. Her interest is not in the patients but in perpetuating her own sense of control, as shown by her apparent dislike of any idea that is not her own. Once McMurphy finds that his proposals will be immediately dismissed, he manipulates the system by using Dr. Spivey. Nurse Ratched is of course infuriated by what it means that Dr. Spivey can talk separately with McMurphy and work with him to make decisions for the ward. This more subtle uprising, the passive-aggressiveness that McMurphy succeeds with, opens a crack in her steel facade. He is winning at the system that Nurse Ratched has been an expert at manipulating against him and the insane people on the ward.

Nevertheless, Chief Bromden emphasizes that no matter what McMurphy gains, his struggles are inevitably in vain. Ultimately, Nurse Ratched has the power of the Combine, a social sanction for any punishment the institution has at its disposal against those who rebel. Ratched has many cards left to play.

Summary and Analysis of Part One, Chapters 10-15

McMurphy plays Monopoly with Harding, Martini, Scanlon, and Cheswick. Martini hallucinates, thinking he sees things on the board. McMurphy keeps high-class manners around the nurses and the boys in spite of what they say to him—in spite of every trick they pull to make him lose his temper. McMurphy also keeps his sense of humor. He continues to see how funny the rules are. As long as he can laugh at the ridiculousness of everything that is happening around him, he will be safe.

Only once does he become visibly angry. At one of the group meetings, he chastises the patients for acting too cagey, for being "chicken-shit." McMurphy wanted to change the schedule around so the men could watch the World Series during the day and do the cleaning work at night. McMurphy expects the nurses to oppose him and his fellows to support him. But when McMurphy attempts to round up a vote for the schedule change, the Acutes fail to see the purpose in doing any such thing. He confronts Harding, whose failure of support suggests to McMurphy that he is afraid of Nurse Ratched. Billy Bibbit claims that nothing they do will be of any use in the long run.

McMurphy claims that he is going to break out of the institution by lifting up the control panel in the tub room and throwing it through the window. He tries to lift it, but it weighs far too much.

The person named Public Relations shows the institution to a visiting doctor. The doctor examines Chief Bromden. Public Relations claims that there must be something wrong with any man who would want to run away from a place as nice as this. The fog gets worse for Chief Bromden. Bromden thinks that McMurphy cannot understand that the fog keeps the patients safe.

One of the patients, Old Rawler, kills himself, creating a dangerous sense of instability in the ward.

Bromden explains where the thick fog comes from. It emanates from the fog machines he saw during the war. The machines obscured the surroundings so that nobody could see anything in front of him. Bromden would get lost in the fog and always find himself returning to the same place. Bromden waits for Nurse Ratched to fog them in again; lately they have been doing it more and more now that McMurphy has fomented the rebellion of Cheswick and Harding to the point where they might actually stand up to the boys.

Ratched discusses with a doctor whether or not McMurphy should be on the ward, since he is upsetting the patients.

During the therapeutic meeting, the group tries to discuss the source of Billy Bibbit's stutter. Billy relates that he flunked out of college because he quit ROTC when he couldn't answer to his own name. He also recalls that the first word that he stuttered was "mama." He flubbed a proposal to a girl because he stuttered. Nurse Ratched tells him that his mother mentioned the girl to whom he proposed—this girl was said to be quite beneath him. McMurphy brings up the World Series again, and Nurse Ratched reluctantly allows one more vote on the matter.

This time he rouses all twenty Acutes to vote for him, but Nurse Ratched claims that this is insufficient, for none of the Chronics vote for him. McMurphy attempts to rouse at least one Chronic to vote for a schedule change, but none responds. Finally, McMurphy approaches Chief Bromden, who raises his hand. But Nurse Ratched now claims that the vote was already decided and the meeting is closed. An hour later, it is time for the World Series. McMurphy stops work and turns on the television. Nurse Ratched becomes angry and turns off the television from the Nurses' Station, but McMurphy remains sitting there. Finally she approaches him and scolds him for not obeying her. Mr. Harding sits down beside McMurphy, and Cheswick, Scanlon, Billy Bibbit, and the other Acutes join him. Chief Bromden also joins them by the television.

Analysis

If One Flew Over the Cuckoo's Nest is a work of social criticism, this section develops points about the role of everyday people in effecting change. Nurse Ratched is not the only obstacle that McMurphy faces. The apathy of the other patients proves a substantial burden to McMurphy, for they do not have the energy to support changes in ward policy that they actually want. In fact, they take Billy Bibbit's position that any action will not really make a difference for them anyway. It could even be counterproductive. It is up to McMurphy to engage in some consciousness-raising among, at least, the Acutes, who might still have a degree of consciousness that can be raised. McMurphy will work to create a solidarity among the patients.

The control panel in the tub room will prove significant later in the novel. In this section, McMurphy's idea of using it to escape foreshadows later events. Although McMurphy cannot lift it, the Chief is one who can.

Chapters Twelve to Fourteen appear in short succession. Two of them contain little more than one paragraph. This structure serves to show the disjointed nature of Chief Bromden's observations. He presents only brief glimpses of events that occur in the institution, none of which contains any great significance. Even the suicide of Old Rawler is largely inconsequential in terms of the plot and atmosphere of the novel, though the later deaths will be consequential for what they signify about the state of the ward. The most important point that Chief Bromden makes in these chapters is that the "insanity" represented by the fog is a comfort for the patients. It allows them to recede from the difficulties of reality. The additional trouble for McMurphy is that reality is what he wants them to confront.

Chief Bromden acts primarily as a narrator who describes external conditions rather than his own psychology. But in Chapter Fifteen, he provides some indication of the origin of his psychological problems. Bromden compares the imaginary "fog machine" of the mental institution to the real fog that apparently surrounded him during wartime as a matter of military tactics. This tale indicates that Chief Bromden likely suffers from some sort of shell-shock caused by his war experience.

We also get a bit of psychological insight into Billy Bibbit. The origin of Billy Bibbit's problems, following a Freudian perspective, is that his mother is not primarily loving but is domineering like a man. She seems to control his every action, being the judge of which woman is appropriate for him to marry. That the first word Billy Bibbit stuttered was "mama" is a clear indication that she is the source of his problems. His mother's apparent collaboration with Nurse Ratched is further evidence that Billy's mother is the source of most of his difficulties. Apparently he cannot escape his mother even in the asylum.

McMurphy takes even further the role of a revolutionary in this chapter. When he rebels against Nurse Ratched by breaking from the established schedule to watch the World Series, McMurphy is abandoning the rules and regulations of the ward. This rebellion occurs, however, only after it is apparent that the supposedly democratic system of voting on the ward is not actually free; Nurse Ratched controls and manipulates the outcomes of the votes. McMurphy cannot win simply by playing by the rules. This is an important point, for it demonstrates that McMurphy is not just an anarchist bent on breaking down any system of governance. He is driven to rebellion by the unfair system around him, one which he could not change from within even if he tried. Note, too, that he does not act with force but with passive resistance, simply continuing to sit after the television is turned off.

Despite Nurse Ratched's claim that the vote is democratic, her tally includes the Chronics, who have no real ability to make the rational choice required in a vote. This tactic ensures that Nurse Ratched can maintain the status quo whenever she wants, despite the obvious support for McMurphy among the Acutes.

When McMurphy breaks from his schedule to watch the World Series, he makes a definitive break from the regime of Nurse Ratched. It is a revolutionary act that threatens to throw the institution into full upheaval. Indeed, others join him in the protest.

The vote for the World Series is also a turning point for Chief Bromden, for it is the first time he reasserts himself as a functioning person. He does this through his vote for McMurphy, the first definitive, responsive action that Chief Bromden has taken during the novel. He continues this pattern when he joins McMurphy and the other Acutes in their protest against Nurse Ratched.

These actions underscore a major theme of the novel, the importance of rational choice. The ability to choose reflects one's status as a rational, functioning human being. Cannot McMurphy insist, at least, on that? One Flew Over the Cuckoo's Nest centers around the conflict between this capability for choice and Nurse Ratched's refusal to allow people to make decisions for themselves. As a matter of social commentary, too many bureaucrats think it is their job to be the experts and the decision-makers for everyone else, and the novel warns us to be wary of such ideas. The general population may be too apathetic, but we do have rational minds and are not crazy, after all.

Summary and Analysis of Part Two, Chapters 16-18

Chapter Sixteen

Everyone keeps his eyes on Nurse Ratched, who occupies the Nurses' Station. For Chief Bromden, the fog has dissipated. One of the boys prods Chief Bromden to continue with his duties, but Bromden will not move until he is physically prodded to clean the staff room.

He goes to the staff room, where Nurse Ratched is holding a meeting. One doctor discusses the "revolution" that occurred minutes before and says that McMurphy is no ordinary man they are dealing with. Another doctor suggests that McMurphy may be simply a shrewd con man and not mentally ill, but another says that McMurphy is sick and definitely a "Potential Assaultive." The doctor worries that McMurphy may attack him during Individual Therapy. One of the doctors, Gideon, finally decides that they are not dealing with an ordinary man, but Nurse Ratched tells him that he is absolutely wrong. She says that McMurphy is not extraordinary, simply a man and just as subject to all the fears and cowardice and timidity as any other man, such that he ultimately can be controlled. One doctor worries that this could take weeks, but Ratched reminds them that they have all the time in the world. McMurphy is committed involuntarily, so he must remain in the hospital as long as they want.

Chapter Seventeen

The patients love knowing that McMurphy "got the nurse's goat the way he said he would." McMurphy becomes more bold and aggressive. He asks Nurse Ratched for the measurements of her breasts, which she tries so hard to conceal. But Nurse Ratched does not lose control again. Bromden thinks that McMurphy may be strong enough to resist the Combine, suggesting at least a stalemate between hero and villain.

Bromden wakes one night to find the ward clean and silent. He gets up and walks over to the window. He looks outside, and for the first time, he seems to really see the outside world. He can see that the hospital is surrounded by countryside. He watches a dog sniffing around outside until Geever, one of the boys, and the Catholic nurse put Chief Bromden back in bed. Bromden dreams about how the nurse goes home and tries to scrub away her birthmarks, aghast that a good Catholic girl has such stains.

Chapter Eighteen

In the group meetings, the other patients bring up longstanding gripes which they had kept buried. They complain that the dorms are locked on the weekends, that they are not allowed to go various places alone, and that they do not have the right to have their own cigarettes. McMurphy notes that Nurse Ratched acts as if she still holds all of the cards up her sleeve.

When the patients make their weekly trip to the pool, McMurphy learns that she really does have insurmountable power over them. The realization comes in a single moment, when McMurphy discusses with a lifeguard how the hospital is better than a jail. The lifeguard points out to him that, at least in jail, a person has a definite release date. The lifeguard, who is also a patient, tells McMurphy that he was picked up for drunkenness and disorderly conduct and has now been in the institution for nearly nine years. McMurphy will be there as long as Nurse Ratched intends to keep him.

The next day, McMurphy surprises everyone by behaving well. That afternoon, in the group meeting, Cheswick complains that he wants something done about the cigarettes and whines that they are treating him like a child. Two of the black boys drag him away to the Disturbed Ward. McMurphy does not say a thing during the meeting. He has chosen to give in because it is the smart thing to do. The next time that the inmates go to the pool, Cheswick immediately dives into the pool after telling McMurphy that he wishes something had been done. He gets his fingers stuck in the grate at the bottom of the pool and drowns.

Analysis

In Chapter Sixteen, the fog that Chief Bromden claims to see symbolizes his lack of lucidity and his inability to assert himself. But once Bromden makes the decision to join the other men in protest of Nurse Ratched, the fog disappears. This decision comes at a cost. By making choices to resist authority, Chief Bromden becomes vulnerable once again to his long-buried feelings. He loses the safety of the fog and embraces the risks and rewards of personal choice and freedom.

Chief Bromden's choice to continue presenting himself as deaf and dumb is a tactic to deflect harassment by Nurse Ratched's henchmen. This deception also enables Chief Bromden to access staff meetings. In comparison with others, Chief Bromden's purported handicap renders him innocuous, allowing him to be the most omniscient narrator because of his access to places others cannot go. McMurphy himself would be a more lucid narrator, but his self-interest in telling his own story would be likely to distort the narrative. It seems better this way, to have McMurphy's character loom large in an observer's mind as almost a mythological hero. It is up to Chief Bromden to take McMurphy's story out of the institution and into the world. Besides, Bromden will end up being in the clichéd situation of being the one survivor able to tell the tale.

The staff meeting is at once ironic and ridiculous because it reveals the outright absurdity of the doctors' diagnoses. The various doctors use tortured doublespeak. They believe his behavior indicates the presence of a sane man, but he also seems potentially explosive precisely because of his sanity in an environment meant for the insane. Nurse Ratched seems almost desperately afraid that McMurphy might be normal, pushing her further towards a diagnosis of him as a psychotic. Indeed, the Nurse believes that his ordinariness in the context of the ward proves he is insane. His kind of relative insanity in the ward proves him more likely to be sane in normal society.

Ratched wants to win this battle. Whether the sexual subtext is still here or this is simply a matter of pride and power, Nurse Ratched insists to the doctors that McMurphy stay in her department. She intends to break McMurphy down by any means and no matter how long it may take. In this, she is a good totalitarian re-educator.

In Chapter Seventeen, sexuality is again a tactic of McMurphy. He questions Nurse Ratched about her breasts. The theme is continued in some sense by Chief Bromden later when he wonders about the birthmarks of the Catholic nurse in relation to the desire for purity. His observations about the Catholic nurse suggest the detrimental effects of sexual repression; unlike the tightly corseted Nurse Ratched, this nurse seems to demonstrate intense guilt and shame about her sexuality. The narrator describes this situation almost entirely in metaphorical terms of "stains," with obvious sexual connotations.

Although McMurphy becomes more bold and authoritative in this chapter, Nurse Ratched remains calm and reassured. She has regained composure because she knows she has control over the situation in the long run. She can determine what happens to McMurphy and whether or not he is ever released from the asylum, so she can tolerate any short-term challenges to her power, even if occasionally he can draw others to his cause.

The changes in Chief Bromden are particular important in this chapter. We awakens, literally and figuratively, and watches the dog outside the window. For the first time in ages, he is truly aware of the outside world. He is acknowledging it and feels in some way a part of it; he is not simply ignoring it or afraid of it. He can conceive of existence outside of the institution in ways that he could not imagine before. No doubt, McMurphy is the primary facilitator of this change.

Chapter Eighteen emphasizes the effects that McMurphy has had on the other men in the institution. Because of McMurphy, these men begin to reassert their rights against Nurse Ratched. But there is a critical difference between Cheswick's complaints and McMurphy's conscious rebellion, for Cheswick cannot modulate his complaints. He refuses to cease his complaints even after they place him in corporeal danger. Although the actual chronology of the events is unclear, it seems that the black boys take Cheswick to Disturbed to administer shock treatment because of his rebellion. This treatment in turn may have rendered Cheswick incoherent, with the subsequent effect that he makes the foolish error of getting his hands stuck in the grate in the swimming pool. But there is a strong possibility that Cheswick's action is suicidal, for his death occurs almost immediately after he jumps in the pool.

Cheswick may feel let down by McMurphy, who has started to play along just when Cheswick has taken the bold step of initiating his own rebellion. Cheswick's death demonstrates the more disturbing consequences of the clarity that McMurphy instills in the other patients: they sense that they can progress beyond their supposed insanity but might not actually be able to handle their progress or the new awakening they are experiencing. As the patients regain the ability to assert themselves and make choices, they also must face the effects of these decisions, and if their past is any indication, they are generally not very able to face the real world.

As for McMurphy, he shows himself to be pragmatic in acquiescing to Nurse Ratched and following her orders. McMurphy rebelled against Nurse Ratched partially because he did not realize her power to control his dismissal from the institution. This power, as earlier established, has given Nurse Ratched the confidence that she will ultimately break McMurphy. McMurphy's change in behavior in this chapter demonstrates that her confidence is well-founded. Moreover, she also has punishments at her disposal, so the next round is likely to lead to another win by Nurse Ratched.

Summary and Analysis of Part Two, Chapters 19-23

Chapter Nineteen

Sefelt, an epileptic, has a seizure during lunch because he refuses to take his medication. Sefelt has been giving his medication to Frederickson. McMurphy asks Frederickson why Sefelt refuses to take his medicine, Dilantin, and he answers that Dilantin makes one's gums rot. The choice is between having his gums rot or having seizures. One of the boys removes two of Sefelt's teeth as Scanlon mentions, "damned if you do and damned if you don't."

Chapter Twenty

The clean, calculated movements of the ward resume as Nurse Ratched reassumes her complete control over the function and operation of the institution.

Chapter Twenty-One

Chief Bromden goes with the Acutes to the library. One of the boys brings Harding's wife into the library. She is as tall as he is and carries a black purse; her fingernails are blood red. Harding introduces McMurphy to his "counterpart and Nemesis." Harding tells his wife, Vera, how McMurphy stood up to Nurse Ratched. She scolds her husband for making a mousy squeak when he laughs. This comment makes Harding nervous and jumpy. Vera then asks for a cigarette, and Harding tells her that the cigarettes have been rationed. This causes a fight between Harding and his wife; she asks whether he ever does have enough, and he asks her in return whether she is speaking symbolically.

McMurphy offers her a cigarette, and she leans forward to take it so that everyone can see down her blouse. Vera complains that Harding's friends, "hoity-toity boys with the nice long hair combed so perfectly and the limp little wrists," keep visiting the house to see him. She suddenly decides to leave. Harding asks McMurphy what he thinks of her, and he replies that she has breasts as big as Nurse Ratched's. McMurphy gets angry when Harding asks for a more serious answer, telling Harding that he has worries of his own and does not want to deal with Harding's. Later, McMurphy admits that he has been suffering from bad dreams over the past week.

Chapter Twenty-Two

Several weeks after the vote on the World Series, the patients are taken to another building to get chest X-rays for tuberculosis. McMurphy sees a room that is unmarked. He asks Harding what happens inside, and Harding tells him that the room is the Shock Shop. Although Harding says that they are witnessing the sunset of electroshock therapy (EST), Nurse Ratched is one of the few remaining advocates of it. Harding claims that EST is not always used for punitive means but "for a patient's own good."

Harding relates the history of EST. It came about when two psychiatrists were visiting a slaughterhouse and watched how a blow to the head would induce an epileptic convulsion in a cow, and they concluded that if a seizure could be induced in non-epileptics, great benefits might result. Harding claims that the process is painless, but the jolt sets off a wild carnival of images.

Harding also mentions lobotomy, which he calls "frontal lobe castration." He says that if Ratched "can't cut below the belt she'll do it above the eyes." McMurphy says that if Nurse Ratched is truly the patients' problem, the solution is to throw her down and penetrate through her sexually repressive defenses. The other patients propose that McMurphy do the job.

McMurphy asks the other patients why they never told him that Nurse Ratched controls whether or not he can leave. Harding says that he forgot that McMurphy was committed involuntarily. Harding tells him that most of the patients are not committed involuntarily, just Scanlon and some of the Chronics. McMurphy asks why Billy is here if he does not have to be—he could be in a convertible "bird-dogging girls." Billy claims that he is too weak to leave and likes it where he is. He then begins to cry as the scars on his wrist open and begin to bleed.

Chapter Twenty-Three

The other patients calm Billy as the patients return to the ward. Chief Bromden walks beside McMurphy and can tell that he is afflicted with some great worry. McMurphy asks Sam, one of the boys, if he can stop by the canteen to get cigarettes. At the canteen, McMurphy buys several cartons. During the meeting that afternoon, Nurse Ratched brings up their behavior several weeks ago. She claims that she waited too long to deal with it and give the men a chance to apologize. She claims that her discipline now is entirely for their own good. She is taking away tub room privileges. McMurphy says nothing. He stands up and walks with his normal swagger to the Nurses' Station and punches the glass in order to get his cigarettes. He sarcastically says that the glass was so clean that he completely forgot it was there.

Analysis

In Chapter Nineteen, Sefelt chooses not to take his medicine because it causes his gums to rot. This is not a psychosomatic fear; gum problems can be real side effects of the medicine. But because Sefelt refuses to take his medicine, he has seizures, ultimately causing him to lose teeth. Sefelt's choice is thus between bad teeth or bad gums, as Scanlon puts it—"damned if you do and damned if you don't." This fatalism is a disappointing condition in the ward. What Scanlon fails to note is that the bad gums are a price to pay for the benefit of reducing seizures, while the bad teeth are tied to the extra troubles of the seizures. The choice should be easy—to take the medicine—but Sefelt chooses badly.

Chapter Twenty, just a paragraph long, marks the change in the ward after McMurphy gives up his struggle against Nurse Ratched. She once again reasserts her control over the rest of the patients, for McMurphy knows that to oppose her is to ensure that he will never leave the ward.

The confrontation between Harding and his wife in Chapter Twenty-One centers almost entirely around their sexual problems. Vera Harding is juxtaposed with Nurse Ratched. They are outwardly similar (especially in McMurphy's eyes) because they both have large breasts, but while Big Nurse is repressed and cold, Vera Harding is imposing in her sexuality. Her blood-red fingernails are a complement and contrast to Nurse Ratched's icy orange polish. Vera Harding intimidates her husband with her sexuality, leaning over to get a cigarette intentionally so that the other patients can see down her blouse. She goes on to complain about her husband's inadequacies, which he perceives as a sexual metaphor, probably correctly. Vera additionally questions her husband's sexual preference, mentioning the boys with "limp wrists" who visit their home—a stereotypical invocation of male homosexuality—who are Harding's friends. Whether or not Harding is a closeted homosexual, Vera seems to be using this idea as a tactic to humiliate her husband by playing on his sexual anxieties.

McMurphy demonstrates some strain in this chapter as well. He seems to be weary of acting as the leader or authority figure for the men on the ward. If Cheswick might have caught a sense of this weariness, it becomes clearer when McMurphy refuses to give his appraisal of the problems between Harding and his wife. McMurphy is under some psychological strain, likely caused by worry that he will never be able to leave the institution.

Harding describes the processes of electroshock therapy and lobotomies in great detail in Chapter Twenty-Two, thus foreshadowing their use. He makes the important point that it is Nurse Ratched who uses these methods, even if they are becoming discredited. Though he notes that such treatment is not always for punitive means, he simultaneously suggests that these methods sometimes actually are used as punishment when Ratched is disobeyed. Harding also uses lobotomies as a metaphor for sexual crippling through "castration" of the frontal lobe. The conversation between McMurphy and Harding once again defines the opposition between McMurphy and Ratched in sexual terms. Nurse Ratched can use lobotomies as the equivalent of castration, while McMurphy suggests sex as the cure for Nurse Ratched's repression and control. McMurphy also puts himself in the role of sexual liberator.

Billy Bibbit's mother seems to control his actions, rendering him weak and at least symbolically impotent. There is a link between Mrs. Bibbit and Nurse Ratched; Billy claims that the two women are close friends. Nurse Ratched thus serves as a stand-in mother who can manipulate Billy Bibbit's weaknesses and insecurities. This vulnerability will become important in future chapters.

When McMurphy realizes that most of the patients have made the choice to remain in the institution, he realizes that personal choice and fear of one's problems in the outside world have put most of the inmates in the asylum. Only he and a small number are actually committed; the others remain under Nurse Ratched's control out of fear or habit. This differentiates McMurphy from the other patients; he is sane because he uses his ability to make rational choices while the other patients are coded as insane through their refusal to take their chances out in the world.

Nurse Ratched has reasserted her control over the institution in Chapter Twenty-Three, again a mother or a warden who dominates the men. She speaks to them in utterly condescending terms, even referring to them as "boys" and treating them as children who cannot accept any sense of responsibility. Having treated these men with such great disrespect and taking away something of value to McMurphy, she triggers his anger. He responds with impudence. When he breaks the glass, this is the first physically aggressive action he takes against Nurse Ratched. This brings the confrontation between the two characters back to the fore, for McMurphy is aggressively acting out on behalf of the privileges of the patients. He is taking a risk in that the act will mean a longer stay in the institution, but at this moment his anger or rebellion is stronger than such a fear.

Summary and Analysis of Part Three, Chapters 24-25

Chapter Twenty-Four

McMurphy has things his own way for a while after the incident with the cigarettes. Nurse Ratched is in no hurry to retaliate because she knows she can prolong the fight as long as she wishes. McMurphy gets together a basketball team and talks the doctor into letting him bring a ball back from the gym to get the team used to handling it. Trying to push the limits, McMurphy requests an Accompanied Pass—to be accompanied specifically by "a switch from Portland named Candy Starr." When this request is turned down, McMurphy breaks the glass again. The other Acutes begin to follow McMurphy's lead in behaving aggressively. Martini accidentally bounces the basketball into the window, breaking it a third time.

McMurphy decides that fishing is the thing to do. He requests a pass after telling the doctor he has some friends at the Siuslaw Bay at Florence who could take several patients deep-sea fishing. He would be accompanied by "two sweet old aunts from a little place outside of Oregon City." McMurphy begins recruiting patients to go, but Nurse Ratched puts up clippings about wrecked boats and sudden storms on the coast in efforts to dissuade the patients.

Chief Bromden wants to go but does not have the money and does not want Nurse Ratched to think that he can hear others. Bromden remembers that he did not start acting deaf; others started acting as if he were too dumb to hear or see anything. Bromden reminisces about his childhood, when men in Stetson hats used to visit the Indian reservation where he lived. These men insulted the Indians in front of Bromden, but when he attempted to speak up, they ignored him.

One night McMurphy finds Chief Bromden awake and talks to him. He wonders where he gets his chewing gum, for Chief Bromden never visits the canteen, but then realizes that the Chief chews already-used gum. McMurphy gives Bromden a new pack of Juicy Fruit; he tries to actually speak the words "Thank you." McMurphy tells Bromden that he once had a job picking beans. Since he was the only kid there, McMurphy never said a word, but he listened intently and, on the last day, revealed all that he heard and created a disturbance. McMurphy wonders if Chief Bromden is doing the same thing, but he admits to McMurphy that he could not tell anyone off like McMurphy does because Bromden is not as big or as tough.

Bromden also tells McMurphy that his father was a full Chief, Tee Ah Millatoona (The Pine That Stands Tallest on the Mountain)—and his mother was twice his size. Bromden says that the Combine worked on his father for years, but his father fought it until his mother made him too little to fight anymore. Bromden wants to touch McMurphy, not because he is "one of those queers" but because of who he is. McMurphy offers to let Chief Bromden go on the fishing trip for free. He wonders if

Chief Bromden could lift the control panel in the tub room. He suggests that the Chief take the opportunity and break out of the institution.

Chapter Twenty-Five

Chief Bromden eagerly awaits the deep-sea fishing trip. He sees that McMurphy signed his name on the list. The black boys wonder who signed Chief Bromden's name, fully convinced that Indians cannot read or write. McMurphy wakes up the others on the ward, trying to gather one more person to go on the trip. George Sorenson, a big, toothless old Swede with a compulsion about sanitation, agrees to go.

Nurse Ratched arrives and attempts to scare the patients once more about the dangers on the ocean. Still, George remains resolved to go, and McMurphy even makes him "captain." Only one of the two chaperones/whores arrives, a girl named Candy, and she is late. She tells McMurphy that Sandra, the other hooker, left and got married. Nurse Ratched does not allow the men to leave because they need another chaperone for so many patients. Dr. Spivey agrees to accompany them.

When the men stop for gas, the service-station man asks if they are from the asylum. The doctor tells him that they are a work crew, not inmates. The service-station man behaves rudely to the men, but McMurphy tells them that they are in fact criminally insane men from the asylum and are entitled to a government-sponsored discount. Harding perceives that mental illness has the aspect of power: the more insane a man is, the more powerful he can become.

When they reach the docks, McMurphy argues with the captain who was supposed to take them out. He demands a signed waiver clearing him with the proper authorities. While McMurphy argues with the captain, a couple of men at the dock yell disparaging comments at Candy, asking whether she is one of the insane or part of the cure for them. McMurphy exits the captain's office and tells the men to quickly get in the boat. They all jump in and push off before the captain gets off the phone.

Candy and Billy Bibbit fish together, and she nearly gets hurt, but everyone laughs at the situation thanks to McMurphy. Dr. Spivey hooks the largest fish, but it takes several men to pull it in. When the men return to shore, the police are waiting for them. The doctor claims that they are a legal, government-sponsored expedition, and he notes that there were not enough life jackets on the boat. The captain thus decides not to press charges. The men who made disparaging comments to Candy say nothing when they return from fishing, for they sense a change in the inmates; these are not the same bunch of "weak-knees from a nuthouse" as before.

On the ride back to the institution, Candy falls asleep against Billy's chest. He later asks her for a date. McMurphy plans to sneak Candy into the ward on Saturday night so she can meet with Billy. McMurphy seems exhausted on the trip back to the institution. He points out the house where he lived as a youth and points out a dress hanging in the branches of a tree. The first girl who dragged McMurphy to bed wore that dress, and it now stands in the tree as a de facto memorial. He was about ten at the time.

Analysis

McMurphy becomes more bold in Chapter Twenty-Four, erroneously believing that Nurse Ratched's failure to retaliate against him indicates that he has won. Instead, however, Nurse Ratched refuses to respond to McMurphy's aggressive stance because she is confident that she will inevitably break him. McMurphy's behavior seems, in fact, a tactical error, for his aggression does not promote self-sufficiency among the patients so much as insubordination. Nurse Ratched essentially gives McMurphy this latitude to allow him eventually to make a grievous error that would justify punishment. Still, the conflict between the two characters remains muted. Nurse Ratched is content with subtle undermining of the fishing trip by putting up clippings of news stories.

Chief Bromden's stories about his childhood suggest that he, like Harding and Billy Bibbit, suffers to some degree from a domineering female. Like Billy Bibbit, Chief Bromden is intimidated by his mother, whom he describes as "twice as tall" as his tall father. Bromden indicates that his mother dominated both him and his father, contributing to the problems they faced. It is from his father that Chief Bromden developed the idea of the Combine. The stories also relate a great deal about his character. He appears to be deaf and dumb primarily because he has been intimidated by others around him, including the callous inspectors or his domineering mother. He has been ignored or disregarded out of racism and other factors, yet he is ready to reassert himself once McMurphy shows him a degree of kindness and respect. Chief Bromden is the best example of the beneficial effect that McMurphy has on the patients in the institution.

The narrator employs foreshadowing again later when McMurphy discusses the control panel in the tub room. McMurphy gives Chief Bromden the idea that he might be able to lift the control panel and throw it through the window, allowing an escape. The reader is coming to believe that Bromden might gain enough wherewithal to do it. The question is what will ultimately motivate Chief Bromden to assert himself so strongly.

The conflict between Nurse Ratched and McMurphy gives way during Chapter Twenty-Five to a different conflict between the institutional patients and the rest of society. Regular human society is not in the institution or out on the water; it is at the gas station and the docks. Upon leaving the institution, McMurphy and the other patients face the suspicion and mockery of those who view them as completely insane. The outsiders are probably more right than wrong, but McMurphy proudly faces these objections through confrontation, celebrating their insanity as a means of intimidation. The good doctor is also on their side, willing to lie when the time comes.

This chapter sets up further plot developments, such as the developing intimacy between Candy Starr and Billy Bibbit.

This chapter also carries strong religious imagery. McMurphy leaves the hospital with twelve followers, an allusion to the twelve apostles of Jesus Christ. Furthermore, their task is deep-sea fishing, another Christian religious symbol insofar as the fish is a prominent symbol of Jesus. The accumulation of these allusions positions R.P. McMurphy as a Christ-figure in One Flew Over the Cuckoo's Nest. If he is a redeemer on the pattern of Christ, the inmates are being invited to cast aside their former selves and find new life in what McMurphy represents—freedom. But following this pattern, McMurphy must at least symbolically die for the men in order to accomplish their final transformation.

The fishing trip itself is a transformative event for the patients. It is a conversion for the men, for they return from their journey changed, now worthy of respect because they seem more sane than insane. The hecklers at the docks no longer mock the patients upon their return from fishing. While McMurphy and the trip itself are agents of the change, the transformation is also due to the patients' physical freedom from Nurse Ratched's control. Freed from her domineering policies, these men do have their own abilities to make their own choices; they can achieve the sense of self-worth that she denies them.

Summary and Analysis of Part Four, Chapters 26-29

Chapter Twenty-Six

Nurse Ratched plans her next maneuver for the day after the fishing trip, just as McMurphy begins hustling for more changes in the rules, including a subscription to *Playboy* to replace the current one for *McCall's*. She pastes up statements of the patients' financial doings over the past several months, suggesting that McMurphy has made money from the rest of the patients. McMurphy does not appear ashamed, however, and he brags that he might be able to retire to Florida with the money he has made. The patients start to wonder, however, what scam McMurphy is trying to pull.

Nurse Ratched capitalizes on these fears and sets up a meeting without McMurphy, at which she implies that he is trying to fleece them of their money and that this is his only motivation in befriending them. She tells them that McMurphy is no martyr or saint but an old-fashioned con artist. Finally, she questions the profit that McMurphy made on the fishing trip. Harding breaks ranks and agrees that Nurse Ratched is correct, but he asks why they should criticize McMurphy when he is showing off his capitalist flair.

When confronted, McMurphy makes no pretense about his motives. Billy is the only one who openly defends McMurphy, but after the meeting McMurphy asks Billy for money for Candy's visit. Chief Bromden still believes that McMurphy is a "giant come out of the sky to save us from the Combine," but Nurse Ratched's arguments make him start to question McMurphy's deeper motives. These doubts deepen when McMurphy has Chief Bromden move the control panel in the tub room to win the bet he had with the other patients--and then gives Chief Bromden part of the profits. When Chief Bromden refuses to take the money, McMurphy confronts him about the cold treatment the patients are giving him. Chief Bromden tells him that the other patients are suspicious about how McMurphy is always winning things and accumulating their money.

Nurse Ratched orders a cautionary cleansing for the patients in which the men must line up nude against the tile of the shower room and be cleaned by the black boys. The boys torment George Sorenson because he refuses soap and then refuses to bend over for a different cleaning treatment, but McMurphy defends Sorenson. Washington, one of the boys, punches McMurphy, kindling a melee between McMurphy and all of the boys. Chief Bromden takes up the fight with one of the boys as McMurphy's new ally, and the two eventually are victorious. The smallest boy manages to run and get help from the Disturbed Ward. Soon help arrives and people take McMurphy and Bromden away.

Chapter Twenty-Seven

There is a high-pitched machine-room clatter on the Disturbed Ward, as well as the singed smell of men going berserk. With all the progressive chaos, a tall bony man tells a black boy, "I wash my hands of the whole deal." A nurse treats McMurphy's and Bromden's wounds and tells them that not every ward is like Nurse Ratched's. The nurse claims that Nurse Ratched tries to run it like an Army hospital, and she believes that all single nurses should be fired after they reach thirty-five. The nurse admits that she sometimes wishes she could keep the men there instead of sending them back to Nurse Ratched.

The next morning, Nurse Ratched asks McMurphy if he is ashamed of what he did, and if he is ashamed he will not receive shock treatment. McMurphy refuses. He says that the "Chinese Commies" could have learned a few things from her. As the doctors put graphite salve on McMurphy's temples, he asks if he gets a crown of thorns. Chief Bromden receives shock treatment too. As he does, he thinks about his parents, but he manages to regain lucidity afterward, and for the first time knows that he has beaten Nurse Ratched.

Chapter Twenty-Eight

McMurphy receives three more treatments that week, even though Chief Bromden tries to talk McMurphy into complying with Nurse Ratched to get out of it. McMurphy jokes that she is merely "charging his battery." The first woman who takes him on will "light up like a pinball machine and pay off in silver dollars." Chief Bromden leaves Disturbed at the end of the week, and Harding congratulates him when he returns.

There are rumors, however, that McMurphy is not responding at all to the EST. Nurse Ratched realizes that McMurphy is quickly becoming a legend while he is out of the ward, so she plans to bring him back to the ward. The men believe that the best thing for McMurphy would be an escape from the ward on Saturday night. During a meeting Nurse Ratched suggests "an operation," and McMurphy jokes that she is considering castration.

Chief Bromden notes that Billy Bibbit, although he looks young, is actually over thirty. Chief Bromden thinks remembers that when Billy's mother visited and Billy asserted his age, she asked, "Do I look like the mother of a thirty-one year old?"

At midnight, Mr. Turkle comes in for his shift, and McMurphy bribes him by offering Candy's services to him. Candy arrives with Sandy, the whore who had skipped the fishing trip. While Candy gives Mr. Turkle wine, McMurphy attempts to pick the lock to the drug room. Meanwhile, other men look through the files in the Nurses' Station. Harding gets pills for Sefelt and imitates a religious ceremony, sprinkling them over Sefelt and Sandy. Harding claims that they are "doomed henceforth," for Ratched will tranquilize them out of existence. Harding's speech makes the men realize the seriousness of what they are doing.

Mr. Turkle unlocks the seclusion room for Billy and Candy. Harding has a plan to tie up Turkle and make it look like McMurphy had tied him up and taken his keys. This plan, according to Harding, would keep the other men out of trouble, keep Turkle his job, and get McMurphy off the ward. McMurphy asks why Harding does not leave, and he responds that he is not ready. He claims that he is guilty and has indulged in certain practices society considers shameful. McMurphy and Sandy snuggle in each other's shoulders, getting comfortable, as McMurphy postpones his departure for another hour or so. The black boys find him when they arrive at six-thirty that morning.

Chapter Twenty-Nine

Chief Bromden realizes that what happened that night was inevitable, even if Mr. Turkle had gotten McMurphy and the two girls off the ward as planned. The black boys herd all the inmates into the day room, Chronics and Acutes alike. Everyone is still in pajamas. Mr. Turkle resigns and leaves with Sandy. Harding tells McMurphy to run away with them, but McMurphy refuses. The boys take roll in reverse alphabetical order to throw people off. Finally they call Billy Bibbit's name, but he is not there. Nurse Ratched does a room check to find him and reaches the Seclusion Room. She finds Billy in bed with Candy.

Nurse Ratched vigorously scolds Billy for being with "a woman like this. A Cheap! Low! Painted," and Harding suggests "Jezebel" or "Courtesan" or "Salome." The other patients laugh at Harding's comment. Nurse Ratched asks Billy what his mother will think about this incident. She claims that Mrs. Bibbit has always been proud of her son's discretion and will be terribly disturbed; Mrs. Bibbit may even become sick from the news. Billy begins stuttering again and shakes, pleading with Nurse Ratched not to tell his mother. Nurse Ratched attempts to reassure him that nobody will harm him, but she will explain it all to his mother. She leads Billy into the doctor's office, then leaves him there alone as she calls the doctor. When the doctor arrives, he finds that Billy has cut his throat.

Nurse Ratched blames McMurphy, telling him that he is playing with human lives, as if he thought himself to be a god. McMurphy attacks Nurse Ratched, ripping her uniform all the way down the front to expose her breasts as he tries to strangle her. The black boys pull him off Nurse Ratched before he can kill her. Afterwards, several patients sign out of the hospital, and Dr. Spivey resigns. Nurse Ratched stays in Medical for a week while a Japanese nurse runs the ward.

When Nurse Ratched returns, Harding asks about McMurphy. She cannot speak, so she writes on a notepad that he will be back. Harding says that she is "full of so much bullshit." Nurse Ratched finds it difficult to get the ward back into shape. Harding signs out, and George transfers to a different ward. Martini, Scanlon, and Chief Bromden are the only members of the group who remain.

After three weeks, McMurphy returns; the black boys wheel him in on a gurney. He has had a lobotomy and is now a Vegetable. Martini and Scanlon cannot recognize McMurphy. That night, Chief Bromden smothers McMurphy with a pillow, putting him out of his misery.

Scanlon tells chief Bromden he has to leave. Chief Bromden then lifts the control panel in the tub room and throws it through the window. Chief Bromden runs away and catches a ride with a Mexican man going north. He may go to Canada, but he will stop along the Columbia to check out Portland and The Dalles. He has been gone a long time.

Analysis

In Chapter Twenty-Six, having initiated the transformation of the men on the ward in the previous chapter, McMurphy now asserts himself as the controlling force on the ward. The men are full converts to McMurphy's ethos, following his lead in behavior. However, Nurse Ratched undermines this force by dividing the men from one another; she exposes McMurphy for his self-interested actions and manipulation.

Her criticism of McMurphy bolsters the religious allusions of the previous chapter: she claims that McMurphy is not a "martyr" or a "saint," just a manipulative con man. The irony of this situation is that she herself manipulates the patients, while McMurphy has remained fairly honest about his intentions and his entrepreneurial spirit.

When Nurse Ratched orders the cleaning of the men on the ward, she demonstrates her omnipotence over the patients' bodies. The procedure is at once invasive and emasculating, an intrusion into the men's bodies, analogous to rape. If the men experienced a transformation from being meek and easily dominated to being more confident and respectable, McMurphy experiences an equally momentous shift in this chapter. McMurphy assumes the role of selfless martyr in this chapter, defending George Sorenson against the invasive cleaning procedures of the black boys. In the past, his decisions generally benefited him monetarily or built his reputation. But this is a time when McMurphy is motivated least by self-interest, for he can gain very little or nothing from defending Sorenson.

Christian symbolism dominates Chapter Twenty-Seven, which more fully completes the analogy between McMurphy and Jesus Christ. "I wash my hands of the whole deal" is a direct allusion to Pontius Pilate, who made a similar comment upon ordering the crucifixion of Christ. McMurphy himself realizes this comparison when he asks whether or not he gets a "crown of thorns," another reference to the crucifixion.

The nurse with whom McMurphy speaks also gives a greater indication of Nurse Ratched's character. The younger nurse suggests that a significant motivation for Ratched's behavior is the fact that she is a bitter, old spinster and has taken out her frustrations on the men on the ward. This point returns to the contrast between the sexuality of McMurphy and the repression of Nurse Ratched. The suggestion is that if Nurse Ratched were sexually satisfied, or at least satisfied with her personal life, she would allow greater freedom on her ward.

Nurse Ratched does gain a victory over McMurphy in this chapter, but whatever victory she has will be short-lived. The shock treatment does not significantly affect Chief Bromden; he quickly regains a sense of lucidity afterward and returns to coherence. More importantly, the nurse who treats McMurphy's wounds makes the important point that other nurses are opposed to Nurse Ratched's behavior. Although Nurse Ratched maintains a tight grip on her particular ward, she is vulnerable within the institutional structure she uses against her patients.

Paralleling the Christian story, McMurphy becomes a martyr in Chapter Twenty-Eight when he refuses to accommodate Nurse Ratched's demands for an apology. McMurphy gains power and authority through receiving the electroshock treatment, just as crucifixion and resurrection demonstrate the divinity of Jesus in Christian teachings. Kesey combines this religious symbolism with the sexual themes that informed the first part of the novel, for McMurphy facetiously claims that the EST increases his sexual potency in that his next conquest will "light up like a pinball machine." Kesey reinforces this theme when McMurphy underscores that Nurse Ratched would advocate castration. The religious parallels and increasing indications of martyrdom cause Nurse Ratched to return McMurphy to the ward, even if she only dimly perceives the depth of what he represents to the other men. His reputation can only grow while he is away; by returning him to the ward she can remind the men that he is not the godlike martyr the inmates have imagined.

McMurphy's supposed final night in the institution continues the pattern of religious and sexual imagery, for Harding imitates a religious ritual when he sprinkles the pills on Sefelt. Kesey gives further psychological analyses of the more significant inmates. Harding admits to McMurphy that he has committed practices that society finds unacceptable, a coded final admission that he is a homosexual, while Chief Bromden details more of Billy Bibbit's past. Mrs. Bibbit has rendered her son a thirty-year-old child; she will not allow him to age precisely because it would reflect that she has aged as well. Billy is thus a perpetual child, dominated by his mother's oppressive behavior. When McMurphy arranges for the meeting between Candy and Billy, McMurphy is emphasizing his role as a sexual liberator.

McMurphy's delay in leaving the ward is an ambiguous event, for although he ostensibly makes a small error by falling asleep, the event is perhaps too convenient. Given the signs of his martyrdom, there is a strong possibility that McMurphy never intended to leave the ward and that his actions are a form of self-sacrifice. There are many reasons for him to go, but there are also important reasons for him to stay.

The final chapter of One Flew Over the Cuckoo's Nest culminates in a pyrrhic victory for Nurse Ratched and a pyrrhic victory for the martyred McMurphy. That is, they both win and both lose. The confrontation between the two characters finally becomes both violent and sexual, having been set up as sexual by the confrontation between Nurse Ratched and Billy Bibbit over the prostitute. Nurse Ratched has used repressive sexuality as a weapon against Billy Bibbit, instilling in him a sense of shame that stems from both religious sexual guilt and his domineering mother. Harding even makes a religious allusion to Jezebel that underscores the religious idea of certain kinds of sexuality as sinful. Yet it is when Nurse Ratched uses Billy Bibbit's mother to instill a sense of shame that she drives him to suicide, showing with unerring finality the cause of Billy's problems.

The religious theme continues as Nurse Ratched chastises McMurphy for playing God and causing the deaths of Cheswick and Billy Bibbit. The irony is that her policies and abuses of power are what drove them to their respective deaths. All of her criticisms of McMurphy can be better applied to Nurse Ratched herself, a vengeful goddess over the ward.

McMurphy's attack on Nurse Ratched is about power and sexuality. He effects a literal and figurative exposing of the Big Nurse. When he attacks her, he exposes her breasts, the one barely suppressed sign of her femininity. This point also relates back to Harding's earlier suggestion that sex is the cure for Nurse Ratched—here it is at least a cure for the men against her. The result of this fight is the final humanization of Nurse Ratched in that everyone learns what McMurphy has known from the beginning: she is human and weak and troubled like everyone else. When she returns to the ward after the fight, she is unable to speak and thus has lost a major sign of her power. While she loses this sign of humanity, she neatly parallels Chief Bromden, who in the course of the novel regains his voice and his humanity.

McMurphy ostensibly loses his battle against Nurse Ratched when she orders a lobotomy for him, but the victory is hollow, for she loses control of the ward as the other patients free themselves of her grip and voluntarily leave the hospital. This is an ultimate win for him and an ultimate loss for her. This circumstance also fits well with the Christian symbolism of the novel; although McMurphy dies for his cause, his disciples leave the hospital to live according to his teachings. They have gained the strength and the freedom to make independent choices as McMurphy proposed that they could.

Chief Bromden best exemplifies the new life McMurphy has enabled. Through the course of the novel he has regained his voice, and he makes the final step toward self-realization when he escapes the ward. By moving the control panel and escaping, Chief Bromden fulfills McMurphy's wishes and reasserts himself as a more or less healthy member of society. He now is in a position to tell the tale of McMurphy's liberation.

Suggested Essay Questions

1. What do Nurse Ratched and McMurphy believe are the keys to defeating one another?

   Answer: Nurse Ratched believes that letting McMurphy know how long he will ultimately stay in the joint without her permission to leave will inevitably force him to behave. McMurphy, meanwhile, believes that contesting Nurse Ratched for power and testing her sexual boundaries will make her "crack."

2. What do the black boys represent?

   Answer: They seem to have no personality other than being vehicles for Nurse Ratched's hatred. They are her henchmen. They represent the dark anger, the overpowering rage, that lies inside of her and exists almost outside of herself after being buried for so long.

3. What is Nurse Ratched's primary technique of manipulation among the men of the ward?

   Answer: She relies principally on emasculation to destabilize them. In the case of Billy Bibbit, for instance, she threatens to tell his mother of his behavior problems. She emasculates Harding by siding with his overbearing, domineering wife.

4. What is the purpose of EST in the context of the patients' individual treatments?

   Answer: Electroshock therapy, as described by Chief Bromden, should be used only in the most extreme cases since it essentially induces seizure in order to clear the brain. But in the case of these inmates, Nurse Ratched uses it as punishment, somehow to "teach." If someone is not responsive, she is willing to take the next step and use lobotomy as punishment.

5. How might the story of McMurphy be understood as a religious metaphor?

   Answer: McMurphy himself recognizes the Christian metaphor of his sacrifice and death for the sake of the other inmates. A number of explicit allusions back up this metaphor. McMurphy takes twelve disciples on the fishing trip, is betrayed by a Judas figure, wears a crown of thorns for his ultimate punishment, and is taken down and essentially killed by a repressive regime. He is a kind of Christ-figure in the novel even if the resurrection is Chief Bromden's and not McMurphy's.

6. Why is Chief Bromden the narrator instead of McMurphy?

   Answer: If McMurphy were the narrator, he could not quite be telling the tell as a fable. He would be empowered to control the path of the narrative--if he were still sane. But Bromden, who has not been lobotomized but freed, recounts McMurphy's story and takes the lesson to the outside world. He becomes the messenger.

7. Chief Bromden believes in the "fog" and the power of the "Combine." Explain both in the context of the book's themes.

Answer: The fog is, on an individual level, a kind of mental dimness or confusion that also represents the thickness of delusion and suffering that prevents the inmates from seeing their true situation and their true selves. The Combine is, on a social level, a repressive institution and all the individual wheels and cogs in it that ensure that the inmates stay quiescent.

8. Does McMurphy forget to leave on the night of his escape, or is it a purposeful self-sacrifice?

Answer: When McMurphy supposedly oversleeps and is discovered, we must question the depth of his motivation to escape. McMurphy has found deep fulfillment in helping the men in the ward, especially Bromden, despite his increasing personal frustration. But he also has been letting his frustration distance himself somewhat from his initial efforts at leadership. McMurphy may well be the kind of person who is immoderate in his desires and who might end up oversleeping even while he might have preferred to escape.

9. What is the place of Nurse Ratched after McMurphy's lobotomy?

Answer: McMurphy has figuratively disrobed Nurse Ratched, disempowering her and because she has been exposed as human. Her power over the men is further broken, despite her clear victory over McMurphy as an individual. "Thoughts are free," but if part of one's brain has been removed, one does not even have much in the way of thoughts. Ratched has been stripped of much of her authority, her credibility in the overall institution has been further eroded, and Bromden finally gains the independence to escape.

10. Is Nurse Ratched the true villain of the story?

Answer: Nurse Ratched is nominally the villain, but she symbolizes a somewhat broken institutional system and the problems of a larger, repressive society that subjugates individualism to conformity. She is part of the Combine, and her place in the machine will likely be taken by another upon her demise. Still, she is particularly cruel at a level beyond that of the other doctors and nurses.

Material Changed from Kesey's Original Novel

After One Flew Over the Cuckoo's Nest was published in 1962, Kesey was sued by an employee of the hospital where Kesey had worked prior to publishing his novel. According to the suit, Kesey had slandered a woman he had worked with by making her character a Red Cross nurse in the novel. Because a lawsuit would have been tremendously burdensome, Kesey simply decided to change the passage rather than fight. As a result of the change, the Red Cross Nurse effectively disappeared from the book and was replaced by the character named Public Relation.

The following passages show how the novel changed.

Original Passage:

> Papa ... stands there waiting, and when nobody makes a move to say anything to him he commences to laugh. Nobody can tell exactly why he laughs; there's nothing funny going on. But it's not the way the Red Cross woman laughs, it's free and loud and it comes out of his wide grinning mouth and spreads in rings bigger and bigger till it's lapping against the walls all over the ward. Not like that fat, wet Red Cross laugh. This sounds real. I realize all of a sudden it's the first laugh I've heard in years.

Revised Passage:

> Papa ... stands there waiting, and when nobody makes a move to say anything to him he commences to laugh. Nobody can tell exactly why he laughs; there's nothing funny going on. But it's not the way that Public Relation laughs, it's free and loud and it comes out of his wide grinning mouth and spreads in rings bigger and bigger till it's lapping against the walls all over the ward. Not like that fat Public Relation laugh. This sounds real. I realize all of a sudden it's the first laugh I've heard in years.

These alterations are very simple: a switch of Public Relation for the Red Cross Nurse, and the removal of the word "wet," which seems more apt for the original nurse.

As the novel progresses, the changes are more complex:

Original Text:

> Ten-thirty the Red Cross lady comes in with the ladies' club, clapping her fat hands at the day-room door. "Oh, let a smile be

your umbrella... Isn't it nice, girls? Clean and cheery? This is Miss Ratched. I chose this ward because it's her ward. She's, girls, just like a mother. Not that I mean age, but you girls understand..." She laughs louder and faster than if it was real, like the sharp, nervous laugh some women make at the table round guests they're uncomfortable with. The Red Cross Lady's underclothes are so tight it bloats her face up when she laughs, makes it round and red as the sun that some first-grader painted and put a big smiling face on it. She's a Jew girl and tells lots of Jew jokes to show us it's okay we're not Jews too. She's got funny blond hair and a brown mustache and no eyebrows at all to speak of, so she's drawn curved lines over her eyes to make do. She conducts these tours—serious women in blazer jackets, nodding as she points out how much things have improved over the years. She points out the TV, the big leather chairs, the sanitary drinking fountains; then they all go have coffee in the Nurses' Station. Sometimes she's by herself and she'll just stand in the middle of the day room and clap her hands (you can hear they're wet), clap them two or three times till they stick, then hold them prayerlike together under one of her chins and start spinning. Spin round and around there in the middle of the floor, looking at the TV, the new pictures on the walls, the sanitary drinking fountain: "Oh, everything is so spanking brand new. How nice. How fun-ny!" What she sees that's so funny she don't ever let us in on, and the only thing I can see funny is her spinning round and around out there like a toy—if you push her over she's weighted on the bottom and straightaway rocks back upright. Like a spinning top. She never looks at the men's faces...

Revised:

Ten-thirty Public Relation comes in with a ladies' club following him. He claps his fat hands at the day-room door. "Oh, hello, guys; stiff lip, stiff lip... Look around, girls; isn't it so clean, so bright? This is Miss Ratched. I chose this ward because it's her ward. She's, girls, just like a mother. Not that I mean age, but you girls understand..." Public Relation's shirt collar is so tight it bloats his face up when he laughs, and he's laughing most of the time I don't ever know what at, laughing high and fast like he wishes he could stop but can't do it. And his face bloated up red and round as a balloon with a face painted on it. He got no hair on his face and none on his head to speak of; it looks like he glued some on once but it kept slipping off and getting in his cuffs and his shirt pocket and down his collar. Maybe that's why he keeps his collar so tight, to keep the little pieces of hair out. Maybe that's why he laughs so much, because he isn't able to keep all the pieces out. He conducts these tours — serious women in blazer jackets, nodding to him as

Material Changed from Kesey's Original Novel

he points out how much things have improved over the years. He points out the TV, the big leather chairs, the sanitary drinking fountains; then they all go have coffee in the Nurses' Station. Sometimes he'll be by himself and just stand in the middle of the day room and clap his hands (you can hear they are wet), clap them two or three times till they stick, then hold them prayerlike together under one of his chins and start spinning. Spin round and around there in the middle of the floor, looking wild and frantic at the TV, the new pictures on the walls, the drinking fountain. And laughing. What he sees that's so funny he don't ever let us in on, and the only thing I can see funny is him spinning round and around out there like a rubber toy—if you push him over he's weighted on the bottom and straightaway rocks back upright, goes to spinning again. He never, never looks at the men's faces...

The principles of the characters, then, are the same, but the details vary somewhat. The Red Cross lady is sharpened by mention of her religion and her brown moustache. Public Relation, on the other hand, seems emasculated by his complete lack of hair. Red Cross Nurse, meanwhile, is always somehow wet and seems to breathe a rarified air. Public Relation, on the other hand, is less sharp. Perhaps in the conversion of Red Cross Lady to Public Relation, Kesey muddied the character. The details seem less trenchant.

A final instance comes in the middle of the novel:

Original Passage:

I hear a silly prattle reminds me of someone familiar, and I roll enough to get a look down the other way. It's the plump Red Cross woman Gwen-doe-lin, with the blond hair the patients are always arguing about is it real blond or not. "I say it's brunette," they'll argue. And I say it's true blond; you ever hear of a good Jewish girl bleaching her hair?" "Yeh, but you ever hear of any blonde what had a dark brown moustache?" The first patient shrugs and nods, "Interesting point." Now she's buck naked except for a little white apron with a red cross on the pocket and red rick-rack on the edges. And I see once and for all (the string cuts into her belly clean out of sight and pulls the apron up short) that she's a definite brunette. Dangling from that apron string she's got half a dozen withered objects, tied by the hair like scalps. She's carrying a little pad and a mechanical pencil inlaid with jewels, taking notes on the pain and hell around her, plans to write a funny novel about it all later. There's a clutch of schoolteachers and college girls and the like hurrying after her. They wear blue aprons and their hair in pin curlers. They are listening to the Jew woman give a brief lecture on the tour.

Revised:

> I hear a silly prattle reminds me of someone familiar, and I roll
> enough to get a look down the other way. It's the hairless Public
> Relation with the bloated face, that the patients are always arguing
> about why it's bloated. "I'll say he does," they'll argue. "Me, I'll say
> he doesn't; you ever hear of a guy really who wore one?" "Yeh, but
> you ever hear of a guy like him before?" The first patient shrugs
> and nods. "Interesting point." Now he's stripped except for a long
> undershirt with fancy monograms sewed red on front and back.
> And I see once and for all (the undershirt rides up his back some as
> he comes walking past, giving me a peek) that he definitely does
> wear one, laced so tight it might blow up any second. And
> dangling from the stays he's got half a dozen withered objects, tied
> by the hair like scalps. He's carrying a little flask of something that
> he sips from to keep his throat open for talking, and a camphor
> hanky he puts in front of his nose from time to time to stop out the
> stink. There's a clutch of schoolteachers and college girls and the
> like hurrying after him. They wear blue aprons and their hair in pin
> curls. They are listening to him give a brief lecture on the tour.

Here again it seems that Kesey was averse to reinventing the character and instead
relied on a simple change of the character from female to male with a few required
changes in the details. The sexual and religious confrontations are gone. Public
Relation seems simply a bloated caricature of grossness.

Author of ClassicNote and Sources

Jeremy Ross, author of ClassicNote. Completed on May 26, 2000, copyright held by GradeSaver.

Updated and revised Soman Chainani, February 19, 2008, and Adam Kissel, June 16, 2008. Copyright held by GradeSaver.

Porter, Gilbert. The Art of Grit: Ken Kesey's Fiction. Columbia, Missouri: University of Missouri Press, 1982.

Kesey, Ken. One Flew Over the Cuckoo's Nest: Critical Edition. New York: Viking, 1973.

Kesey, Ken. One Flew Over the Cuckoo's Nest. New York: Viking, 1962.

"One Flew Over the Cuckoo's Nest." 2008-03-20.
<http://kclibrary.nhmccd.edu/kesey.html>.

"Vocabulary: Classic Texts." 2008-03-04.
<http://www.vocabulary.com/VUctcuckoo.html>.

"One Flew Over the Cuckoo's Nest." 2008-03-05.
<http://books.google.com/books?id=R1avIGuqvuMC&dq=&pg=PP1&ots=xgh0HaumAr&si;

Essay: Treatment of the Theme of Power in Ken Kesey's 'One Flew Over The Cuckoo's Nest'

by Daniel James Wood
September 18, 2004

Power is the predominant theme of Ken Kesey's 'One Flew Over The Cuckoo's Nest': who holds power, who doesn't, who wants it, who loses it, how it is used to intimidate and manipulate and for what purposes, and, most especially, how it is disrupted and subverted, challenged, denied and assumed. On a deeper level, the theme reveals the ways in which an individual in pursuit of power will reduce any others who threaten that pursuit to the level of disposable commodities, and this dichotomy is, in turn, embodied in the chaotic relationship shared between Nurse Ratched and her adversary, Randle Patrick McMurphy.

Before McMurphy arrives at the hospital, Nurse Ratched's routine works efficiently in maintaining a simple sense of order. "The ward is a factory for the Combine," 'Chief' Bromden notes in his narration. "It's for fixing up mistakes made in the neighborhoods and in the schools and in the churches... When a completed product goes back out into society, all fixed up good as new, better than new sometimes, it brings joy to the Big Nurse's heart; something that came in all twisted and different is now a functioning, adjusted component, a credit to the whole outfit and a marvel to behold." However, this efficiency exists not in the hospital as a whole, but only within the walls of Nurse Ratched's ward. "You may sometimes get the impression," Harding later tells McMurphy, "having lived only on our ward, that the hospital is a vast efficient mechanism that would function quite well if the patient were not imposed on it." Certainly the routine described by Bromden in the fourth chapter of part one is evidence enough of this claim: each inmate is assigned a job and is to abide by Nurse Ratched's strict schedule, and each inmate fulfills his duties without question and with hardly an upset in that schedule - until McMurphy arrives. "[He has] a marked disregard for discipline and authority," the hospital staff are told. "Time and again he has acted out his hostilities against authority figures - in school, in the service, in jail!" And with McMurphy's disruptive presence entering the machine of the hospital, the conflict begins.

It is clear from the outset that Nurse Ratched holds power over the ward: "We are victims of a matriarchy," Harding tells McMurphy shortly after McMurphy arrives. That they are living under a strict regime is evident in the way each inmate in the ward is labeled as either an 'Acute' or a 'Chronic' and, likewise, in the way Nurse Ratched is referred to simply as the 'Big Nurse.' As such, she holds her power not necessarily for any one characteristic reason and not only because of the things she does, but more importantly she holds power for a functional reason, because of the role she plays. She is the nurse, and she is in charge, and the inmates are simply objects in the machine, Acutes and Chronics, and she does not treat them as individual people, perhaps because none of them particularly stands out as an individual. But that cannot be said of McMurphy, and so he quickly sets to work on undermining Nurse Ratched's power and her regime, resulting in a re-establishment of her power on a characteristic level rather than a functional one - that is, she is forced to re-establish power by way of the deeds she carries out rather than by the role she plays - and McMurphy necessitates this change by reinstating into the ward the one thing she has removed that is in possession of a power comparable to her own: laughter.

"I never saw a scareder-looking bunch in my life than you guys," he tells the inmates. "[You're] even scared to open up and laugh. You know, that's the first thing that got me about this place, that there wasn't anybody laughing... Man, when you lose your laugh, you lose your footing... A man go around lettin' a woman whup him down till he can't laugh any more, and he loses one of the biggest edges he's got on his side. First thing you know, he'll begin to think she's tougher than he is." And he succeeds in bringing laughter back to the ward: "I forget sometimes what laughter can do," the Chief says. Later he remarks on McMurphy's use of humor as a weapon against the routine of the ward: "He begins to see how funny the whole thing is - the rules, the disapproving looks they use to enforce the rules... [and] he goes to laughing, and this aggravates them no end. He's safe as long as he can laugh, he thinks, and it works pretty fair."

Of course, Nurse Ratched cannot play McMurphy's game. McMurphy's laughter is a result of his increasing familiarity with the machine of the ward, so, to regain her diminished power over him, she sets about disrupting his role within that machine. A suggestion goes around the ward that she will send him up to Disturbed - but she changes the rules to reassert her power over the ward as a whole, and she leaves him be. "I've seen [Nurse Ratched] send men half the size of McMurphy up to Disturbed for no more reason than there was a chance they might spit on somebody," says Bromden, "[and] now she's got this bull of a man who's bucked her and everybody else on the staff, a guy she all but said was on his way off the ward earlier this afternoon, and she says no." She says no because she understands the mechanics of power play: "Would removing him undo the harm that has been done to our ward?" she asks. "I don't believe it would... I believe if he were sent to Disturbed now it would be exactly what the patients expect. He would be a martyr to them."

What she does not count on is that McMurphy understands the rules of power play as well. He, too, refutes her expectations, and begins to play obediently by her rules - "he surprised everybody on the ward by getting up early and polishing that latrine till it sparkled" - but, in retaliation, she refutes his expectations of recognizing this change in his behavior. "She acted like it was nothing surprising at all." In this instance there is a power structure at work that is of a more moral nature than the power structure that was in place when McMurphy arrived in the ward - it is the power of a character and his or her characteristic tendencies rather than the power of a person who fulfils a function. Here, we have a structure in which McMurphy sets the rules of disruption, which are then built upon by Nurse Ratched when she chooses not to fulfill her responsibilities in terms of resolving that disruption, built upon again by McMurphy choosing to voluntarily resolve the disruption he caused, built upon once more by Nurse Ratched not acknowledging this resolution. McMurphy gains the upper hand as a result of this structure: he puts Nurse Ratched in a position where she can either turn down the opportunity to acknowledge his voluntary resolution of his own disruption and, in so doing, acknowledge his power to wound or heal the ward as he sees fit, or she can not acknowledge his voluntary resolution and, as a result, become a more antagonistic figure than she was before the conflict even began; either way, she loses. "[Some of the inmates] figure he's letting her relax," says Bromden, "then he's going to spring something new on her, something wilder and more ornery than ever." This is certainly his tactic; he plays Nurse Ratched the way he plays his poker games: "he dealt and talked and roped [the men] in and led them smack up to the point where they were just about to quit, then [he] backed down a hand or two to give them confidence and bring them along again." The power belongs to McMurphy, and Nurse Ratched is his pawn no matter what she does.

However, although the battle between them is rooted in their deeds, the heart of their conflict is rooted in their principles. Nurse Ratched does not care why certain rules have been established - indeed, her excuse for every rule is that it is simply for the therapeutic benefit of the patients - but instead she cares only that certain rules have been established, and must be abided by. Likewise, in the incident with the re-arrangement of the television schedule to accommodate the World Series, McMurphy ultimately does not care what he watches on television, but instead cares only that he watches television. It is a matter of principle - as long as he can change the rules she has established, even if he does not succeed in changing them as much as he had hoped, he wins the power. When the pressure becomes too intense for her to handle it, she responds in the only way she can: she relents, and she sends McMurphy up to Disturbed for electroshock therapy. But once again, even though she holds the power over him physically, he is still superior to her: by forcing her to resort to sending him to Disturbed, he has made her break the vow she earlier made, and even then he still withstands the treatment she inflicts upon him and, initially at least, he laughs in the face of it; laughter is still his weapon of subversion.

But he stands alone against Nurse Ratched until he can bring the other inmates over to his side. This is the next step in McMurphy's methods of subverting Nurse Ratched's power. If laughter is the only truly successful method of subverting that power and thus rendering the strictness of Nurse Ratched impotent, McMurphy is faced with the task of making the other men laugh, which proves difficult for him to do within the confines of the ward; hence the necessity of the outdoors fishing trip. "Maybe [McMurphy] couldn't understand why we weren't able to laugh yet," says Bromden, "but he knew you can't really be strong until you can see a funny side to things." However, McMurphy's ability to make the men 'loosen up' and laugh comes before they even reach the boat: "Never before did I realize that mental illness could have the aspect of power, power," says Harding, after the incident at the gas station en route to the fishing trip. "Think of it: perhaps the more insane a man is, the more powerful he could become." Later, still speaking of McMurphy, Bromden says: "He knows you have to laugh at the things that hurt you just to keep yourself in balance, just to keep the world from running you plumb crazy." The fishing trip is the perfect remedy for helping the inmates to unwind, and on their return journey to the hospital the fishermen who insulted them earlier in the day "could sense the change that most of us were only suspecting; these weren't the same bunch of weak-knees from a nuthouse that they'd watched take their insults on the dock this morning." McMurphy gives them the means to laugh, but it is not until later that he gives them the motive - after the two prostitutes arrive at the hospital in secret.

When the secret is revealed, Nurse Ratched's power over the men is completely eliminated: her rules have been disregarded to the point of obliteration, and her routine and regime have both been interrupted by the events of the previous night. "When the nurse found the pile of pills Harding had sprinkled on Sefelt and the girl," says Bromden, "we started to pop and snort to keep from laughing." Things take a turn for the worse for Nurse Ratched when one of her own staff is found embroiled in the disruptive activities: "By the time they found Mr. Turkle in the linen room and led him out blinking and groaning... we were roaring." Ultimately the laughter brought about by McMurphy reaches the point where Nurse Ratched can no longer tolerate it with the same kind of stoicism with which she earlier tolerated his abrupt change in behavior: "The Big Nurse took our good humor without so much as a trace of her little pasted smile; every laugh was being forced right down her throat till it looked as if any minute she'd blow up like a bladder... The men were immune to her poison. Their eyes met hers; their grins mocked the old confident smile she had lost." Later, after McMurphy's attack on Nurse Ratched, Bromden notes the accomplishment of the very goal McMurphy was working toward all along: "She couldn't rule with her old power any more."

Although Nurse Ratched does eventually destroy McMurphy, her methods of doing so have less to do with characteristic power and more to do with functional power; she beats him by way of an unfair advantage, and the superiority she achieves over him is only achieved by utilizing resources far beyond McMurphy's grasp. As such, he still retains his power over her, even in his absence, because she was unable to beat him at his own game. If power is the theme of the novel, and laughter the currency in which it is dealt, then McMurphy leaves Nurse Ratched utterly bankrupt: though she removes him from her ward, he removes the perpetual smile from her face and allows the other inmates to wear one on theirs instead. Despite his absence, his presence still lingers and holds some influence over the men in the ward, and that power of longevity and perhaps even martyrdom is of a variety altogether more compelling and more enduring than anything Nurse Ratched is ever able to hold.

Essay: The Presence of Christ in "One Flew Over the Cuckoo's Nest"

by Anonymous
December 03, 2004

R.P. McMurphy is not an average mental patient stuck on a ward at an institution. In fact, McMurphy is one of the most unique patients the ward in "One Flew Over the Cuckoo's Nest" has ever seen. While most of the men on the ward committed themselves, McMurphy opted to be placed in the institution in lieu of fulfilling his sentence to spend time on a work farm. McMurphy is a burly man, with remarkable confidence. The other men idolize him and fear him all from the very first moment that they spend in his presence. At the beginning of the book, McMurphy toys with Big Nurse and the other staff at the hospital. He figures he might as well have some fun with them, since he is under the mistaken impression that he has only "x" number of days until he is released. Soon, however, he comes to realize that he is at Big Nurse's mercy if he ever wants to be free again. Prior to this realization he was an inspiration, someone that others were in awe of and attempted to emulate. When McMurphy realizes that he is destroying his own chance to be free and continues down this path anyway, he effectively becomes the savior of the ward. Like Christ's decision to die for the sins of man, McMurphy gives himself up for the freedom of the other men on the ward.

On several occasions throughout the book, the similarities between McMurphy and Christ are revealed through McMurphy's interactions with the other men in the ward. For example, when McMurphy takes Chief by the hand and tells him that he will make him whole again, the scene's imagery alone serves as a reference to Christ. McMurphy makes Chief, a Native American with a broken spirit and rampant insecurities, his project, embodying all who need to be saved. At one point, McMurphy grips Chief by the hand and Chief, deluded though he may be, feels that McMurphy's blood is pumping directly into his own arm. It seems to Chief like McMurphy is literally giving up his own blood to make him whole again.

Later in the book, another example of McMurphy's Christ-like behavior in the presence of Chief occurs when Chief is admiring McMurphy's arms, commenting on the fact that they are similar to how his own were when he played football as a young man. Chief is in awe of McMurphy, and thinks, "I ought to touch him to see if he's still alive." Once again, this is a scene in which McMurphy's character is heavily influenced by Christ. Chief comments on the similarity between McMurphy's arms and his own, recalling how Christ was created in the likeness of man. People are encouraged to see Christ in themselves and in each other: He was brought into this world a mere mortal so that He could spread The Word in a way mankind could easily relate to. McMurphy is just a man, like any of his friends on the ward.

At another point in "One Flew Over the Cuckoo's Nest", Chief emulates the "doubting Thomas" reaction to the resurrection of Christ. He feels that he must be in physical contact with McMurphy in order to believe in him; this recalls Thomas' need to place his hand in Christ's wounds to feel for himself that the holes are real.

McMurphy's cross is not an easy one to bear: although he is not wholly accepting of his fate, he is aware of it. He knows that if he continues on as he has thus far, he will become the primary focus of Big Nurse. The men will be free to witness his strength and her weakness, and will therefore grow as men and as people, free to take pride in their lives. Each time he is called in for shock treatments "he pale[s] and dread flicker[s] across his face". In this moment, he is saying in his own way that "if this is what needs to be done for them then so be it, but I wish that wasn't the case".

Before he was betrayed by Judas, Christ went to the Garden of Gethsemane, where he fell to his knees and prayed to God to allow him to avoid the death he knew was forthcoming:

"O My Father, if it is possible, let this cup pass from Me; nevertheless, not as I will, but as You will. O My Father, if this cup cannot pass away from Me unless I drink it, Your will be done."

Like Christ, McMurphy knows what has to be done, but does not necessarily want to go forward to do it. McMurphy has not had a particularly enjoyable path in life: Christ was forced to carry a cross and wear a crown of thorns, and McMurphy has endured hours of shock treatment and a lobotomy. Both of these men save others by enduring unthinkable torture.

The deaths of Christ and McMurphy are also more similar than one might initially think. When Christ died, he set mankind free. Many believe that Christ's death will allow mankind to enjoy eternal life. His death was a gift for the world, but release from the torment he endured was a gift to Him, as well. McMurphy's death is a gift for him, because he will not spend the rest of his life as a puppet for Big Nurse. It is also a gift for the other men on the ward, because McMurphy dies trying to show them the best way to live.

The correlations between Christ and McMurphy abound throughout "One Flew Over the Cuckoo's Nest". Throughout the novel, Kesey references this connection through numerous images, events, and interactions. McMurphy frequently proves himself worthy of his status as a savior. In the end, he truly does set the men on the ward free, granting them life just as Christ did for all mankind.

Quiz 1

1. **Which of the following is not a domineering mother figure in the novel?**
   A. Nurse Ratched
   B. Mrs. Bibbit
   C. Mrs. Bromden
   D. Vera Harding

2. **What is Nurse Ratched's only incongruous physical trait?**
   A. Her smooth skin
   B. Her orange nail polish
   C. Her large breasts
   D. Her full lips

3. **Which of the following does McMurphy represent the least?**
   A. Anti-social behavior
   B. Rational choice
   C. Insanity
   D. Sexual liberation

4. **Which character calls the patients rabbits who need a strong wolf?**
   A. Nurse Ratched
   B. R.P. McMurphy
   C. Dale Harding
   D. Billy Bibbit

5. **What is significant about Dr. Spivey's suggestion about the tub room?**
   A. It shows that McMurphy is only interested in games and gambling.
   B. It shows that the doctors do not care about the welfare of the patients.
   C. It shows that Nurse Ratched controls the actions of the doctors.
   D. It shows that McMurphy is as capable as Nurse Ratched of manipulating the system.

6. **Which of the following games do the patients not play?**
   A. Monopoly
   B. Backgammon
   C. Basketball
   D. Cards

7. **What represents insanity for Chief Bromden?**
    A. Nurse Ratched
    B. The Combine
    C. Chewing Gum
    D. The Fog

8. **Which character is most likely a closeted homosexual?**
    A. Nurse Ratched
    B. Dale Harding
    C. Billy Bibbit
    D. Chief Bromden

9. **Which is not an objection that a patient has about Nurse Ratched's policies?**
    A. The loud music
    B. The rationing of cigarettes
    C. The impossibility of getting an Accompanied Pass
    D. The locking of the dormitories on the weekends

10. **Which character has been a patient on the ward the longest?**
    A. Cheswick
    B. R.P. McMurphy
    C. Colonel Matterson
    D. Chief Bromden

11. **Who tells McMurphy that Nurse Ratched determines when he leaves the institution?**
    A. Geever
    B. A Lifeguard
    C. Washington
    D. Dale Harding

12. **When is the first instance in which McMurphy becomes angry?**
    A. When Nurse Ratched refuses to turn down the music.
    B. When the black boys take McMurphy's clothes.
    C. When he learns that Nurse Ratched controls when McMurphy may leave.
    D. When the patients refuse to support his plan for a schedule change.

13. **Which character suffers from intense feelings of Catholic guilt and shame?**
    A. Nurse Ratched
    B. Dale Harding
    C. Billy Bibbit
    D. Nurse Pilbow

14. **What is significant about the origin of Billy Bibbit's stutter?**
    A. It shows that the cause of Billy Bibbit's problems is his mother.
    B. It shows that Billy Bibbit suffers from feelings of sexual inadequacy.
    C. It shows that Billy Bibbit is a closeted homosexual.
    D. It shows that Nurse Ratched causes more problems than she solves.

15. **Why does Nurse Ratched usually not respond harshly to McMurphy's rebellion against her?**
    A. She knows that she can send McMurphy to another ward whenever he becomes too problematic.
    B. She is intimidated by McMurphy and can only respond through indirect means.
    C. She is secretly planning to lobotomize McMurphy.
    D. She knows that she ultimately controls his fate and can determine his release.

16. **What criterion does Nurse Ratched use to determine who works on her ward?**
    A. Physical size
    B. Cruelty
    C. Fear
    D. Anger

17. **For which crime is McMurphy not arrested?**
    A. Disturbing the Peace
    B. Statutory Rape
    C. Public Indecency
    D. Assault and Battery

18. **Which of the characters is not a war veteran?**
    A. Charles Cheswick
    B. R.P. McMurphy
    C. Colonel Matterson
    D. Chief Bromden

19. **To what does Harding compare the patients?**
    A. Chickens at a pecking party
    B. Rabbits
    C. Cows at a slaughterhouse
    D. Sheep

20. **Which of the following sentences about Tee Ah Millatoona is not true?**
    A. He married a town woman.
    B. He was a full Indian chief.
    C. His name means "Stands With a Fist."
    D. His wife drove him to alcoholism.

21. **What is significant about the patients' encounter at the gas station?**
    A. It shows the patients that they cannot escape Nurse Ratched, even outside of the hospital.
    B. It shows the patients the power that their mental illness gives them.
    C. It shows the patients how McMurphy is ashamed of associating with them.
    D. It shows the patients how they are unable to deal with the outside world.

22. **Which of the following does not match the character to his appropriate trait?**
    A. Charles Cheswick - bull goose loony
    B. George Sorenson - compulsive about cleanliness
    C. Dale Harding - hallucinates about air raids
    D. Billy Bibbit - stutterer

23. **Which bet does McMurphy not make with the other patients?**
    A. He bets that a person can move the control panel in the tub room.
    B. He bets that he can get Chief Bromden to speak.
    C. He bets that he can hit the clock with a dab of butter.
    D. He bets that he can get Nurse Ratched to show some sign of weakness within a week.

24. **Which character describes his mother as twice as tall as his father?**
    A. Charles Cheswick
    B. Dale Harding
    C. Billy Bibbit
    D. Chief Bromden

25. **Which of the following is not a reason for Nurse Ratched's confidence?**

    A. She has "the Combine" supporting her.

    B. She knows that the other nurses on other wards will back up whatever she does.

    C. She knows that she controls McMurphy's fate.

    D. She has the power to use procedures such as lobotomies and EST against McMurphy.

Quiz 1 Answer Key

1. **(D)** Vera Harding
2. **(C)** Her large breasts
3. **(C)** Insanity
4. **(C)** Dale Harding
5. **(D)** It shows that McMurphy is as capable as Nurse Ratched of manipulating the system.
6. **(B)** Backgammon
7. **(D)** The Fog
8. **(B)** Dale Harding
9. **(C)** The impossibility of getting an Accompanied Pass
10. **(D)** Chief Bromden
11. **(B)** A Lifeguard
12. **(D)** When the patients refuse to support his plan for a schedule change.
13. **(D)** Nurse Pilbow
14. **(A)** It shows that the cause of Billy Bibbit's problems is his mother.
15. **(D)** She knows that she ultimately controls his fate and can determine his release.
16. **(D)** Anger
17. **(C)** Public Indecency
18. **(A)** Charles Cheswick
19. **(B)** Rabbits
20. **(C)** His name means "Stands With a Fist."
21. **(B)** It shows the patients the power that their mental illness gives them.
22. **(A)** Charles Cheswick - bull goose loony
23. **(B)** He bets that he can get Chief Bromden to speak.
24. **(D)** Chief Bromden
25. **(B)** She knows that the other nurses on other wards will back up whatever she does.

Quiz 2

1. **Which of the following patients is not considered a Chronic?**
    A. Ruckly
    B. Bancini
    C. Scanlon
    D. Chief Bromden

2. **What is significant about Billy Bibbit's age?**
    A. Billy's mother is actually only fifteen years older than he is.
    B. Billy is by far the youngest man on the ward.
    C. Billly has spent half his life in the institution.
    D. Billy is actually much older than his appearance and demeanor suggest.

3. **What was Mrs. Bibbit's objection concerning the woman Billy proposed to?**
    A. The woman was underage.
    B. The woman was a Catholic.
    C. The woman was a vulgar, painted Jezebel.
    D. The woman was beneath him.

4. **What is significant about the financial statements that Nurse Ratched posts?**
    A. They suggest that McMurphy has been gambling away all of the patients' money.
    B. They suggest that McMurphy operates primarily out of self-interest.
    C. They show that McMurphy is officially an indigent.
    D. They suggest that McMurphy has secretly been stealing from the patients.

5. **Which of the following does not support the theme that McMurphy is a Christ-figure?**
    A. The comment, "Do I get a crown of thorns?"
    B. The comment, "I wash my hands of the whole deal."
    C. The fishing trip.
    D. The overturning of the gambling table.

6. **Which of the following comments does not support the theme of Nurse Ratched as a force for sexual oppression?**
    A. "I guess if she can't cut below the belt she'll do it above the eyes."
    B. "The solution to all your problems would be to just throw her down and solve her worries, wouldn't it?"
    C. "You can go, Mr. Taber, if you don't wish to take your medication orally."

D. "A cheap! Low! Painted!"

7. **What is significant about McMurphy being characterized as a psychopath?**
    A. It emphasizes that others diagnosed McMurphy as such because he is sexually threatening.

    B. It proves that McMurphy is actually feigning mental illness to get out of farm work.

    C. It shows that any normal person could be considered a psychopath.

    D. It describes characteristics of psychopathy that are better suited to Nurse Ratched.

8. **Which character is described as "a veritable angel of mercy . . . unselfish as the wind"?**
    A. Nurse Ratched
    B. Mrs. Bibbit
    C. R.P. McMurphy
    D. Candy Starr

9. **Where is Chief Bromden's final destination after escaping the institution?**
    A. Mexico
    B. Portland
    C. The Dalles
    D. Canada

10. **What is significant about Nurse Ratched encountering McMurphy when he is wearing only a towel?**
    A. Nurse Ratched enters the shower room without asking permission, showing that she has no respect for the patients' personal space.

    B. Nurse Ratched is notably affected by the confrontation, showing that even she cannot fully repress her sexual urges.

    C. McMurphy makes veiled threats of rape against Nurse Ratched.

    D. McMurphy is wearing shorts under the towel, showing that he planned the confrontation.

11. **Which character laments, "Lord, to think of the chasm of apathy in which we have fallen--a shame, a pitiful shame"?**
    A. Nurse Ratched
    B. Dr. Spivey
    C. R.P. McMurphy
    D. Dale Harding

12. **Who says, "a man that would want to run away from a place as nice as this, why, there'd have to be something wrong with him"?**
    A. Nurse Ratched
    B. Dr. Spivey
    C. Public Relation

D. The Red Cross Nurse

13. **Which diagnosis is not suggested as a possible explanation for McMurphy's apparently psychopathic behavior?**
    A. Potential Assaultive
    B. Latent Homosexual with Reaction Formation
    C. Negative Oedipal
    D. Manic Depressive

14. **Which of the following is not part of Chief Bromden's hallucinations?**
    A. The night-time dissections
    B. The fog machine
    C. The clock
    D. The paper bag

15. **Why does Harding not want to leave the ward with McMurphy?**
    A. He is too afraid of risking Nurse Ratched's retaliation.
    B. He fears how people outside of the ward will perceive him.
    C. He wants to be the "bull goose loony" once again.
    D. He wants to leave the proper way so that everybody knows that he can.

16. **Who do the fog and Combine appear to most regularly?**
    A. Nurse Ratched
    B. Harding
    C. McMurphy
    D. Chief Bromden

17. **Which patient is tormented by his domineering wife?**
    A. Nurse Ratched
    B. Harding
    C. Bibbitt
    D. McMurphy

18. **Who agrees to go at the last minute on the fishing trip, giving the group enough to go?**
    A. Harding
    B. George Sorensen
    C. Jeff Litern
    D. Billy Bibbit

19. **What does McMurphy say Chief Bromden should use to escape?**
    A. Tub through the window
    B. A tunnel through the cafeteria
    C. A fire alarm
    D. A rooftop corridor

20. **What do McMurphy and the group want to watch on TV, setting off a firestorm with Nurse Ratched?**
    A. The presidential election
    B. The World Series
    C. The moon landing
    D. The Oscars

21. **What is the first thing the black henchmen want to do to McMurphy when he arrives?**
    A. Steal his money
    B. Brand him
    C. Give him a shower
    D. Give him food

22. **What does Nurse Ratched lose at the end of the novel?**
    A. Her voice
    B. Her money
    C. Her position
    D. Her car

23. **Who ultimately escapes from the ward?**
    A. Nurse Ratched
    B. Red Cross Nurse
    C. McMurphy
    D. Chief Bromden

24. **What is the name of the electroshock room?**
    A. Shock Cage
    B. Shock Shed
    C. Shock Shop
    D. Shock Store

25. **Who commits suicide toward the end, prompting McMurphy's final rebellion?**
    A. Nurse Ratched
    B. Harding
    C. Bibbit
    D. Chief Bromden

Quiz 2 Answer Key

1. **(C)** Scanlon
2. **(D)** Billy is actually much older than his appearance and demeanor suggest.
3. **(D)** The woman was beneath him.
4. **(B)** They suggest that McMurphy operates primarily out of self-interest.
5. **(D)** The overturning of the gambling table.
6. **(C)** "You can go, Mr. Taber, if you don't wish to take your medication orally."
7. **(A)** It emphasizes that others diagnosed McMurphy as such because he is sexually threatening.
8. **(A)** Nurse Ratched
9. **(D)** Canada
10. **(D)** McMurphy is wearing shorts under the towel, showing that he planned the confrontation.
11. **(D)** Dale Harding
12. **(C)** Public Relation
13. **(D)** Manic Depressive
14. **(D)** The paper bag
15. **(D)** He wants to leave the proper way so that everybody knows that he can.
16. **(D)** Chief Bromden
17. **(B)** Harding
18. **(B)** George Sorensen
19. **(A)** Tub through the window
20. **(B)** The World Series
21. **(C)** Give him a shower
22. **(A)** Her voice
23. **(D)** Chief Bromden
24. **(C)** Shock Shop
25. **(C)** Bibbit

Quiz 3

1. **What does Nurse Ratched do to ultimately punish McMurphy?**
   A. Order him a lobotomy
   B. Make him pay a heavy fine
   C. Send him back to jail
   D. Bar him from the ward

2. **What was the Red Cross Nurse changed to in the process of Kesey's drafting?**
   A. Nurse Ratched
   B. Harding
   C. Dr. Spivey
   D. Public Relation

3. **What does McMurphy complain about as being too loud in the common room?**
   A. The nurse's laughter
   B. The Chronics' moaning
   C. Harding's stuttering
   D. The music

4. **Who does Nurse Ratched threaten to tell about Billy's exploits with the whore?**
   A. Billy's father
   B. Billy's mother
   C. Billy's daughter
   D. Billy's wife

5. **Who helps McMurphy overwhelm the black boys in the shower?**
   A. Nurse Ratched
   B. Harding
   C. Bibbit
   D. Chief Bromden

6. **What does Nurse Ratched do to dissuade the men from going on the fishing trip?**
   A. Sends spies to watch them
   B. Punishes anyone who goes
   C. Puts poison in their food
   D. Posts scary articles about fishing disasters

7. **Who does McMurphy arrange for the men to meet on their fishing trip?**
   A. Whores
   B. The mayor
   C. Their kids
   D. Cigarette salesman

8. **Who continues to rack up the most money in the ward games?**
   A. Nurse Ratched
   B. Harding
   C. Bibbitt
   D. McMurphy

9. **What is the name of the fat, bloated man who comes down the ward occasionally to greet the inmates?**
   A. Red Cross Nurse
   B. Dr. Spivey
   C. Public Relation
   D. Dr. Ratched

10. **What do Dr. Spivey and McMurphy seem to collaborate on when they reminisce about their school experiences?**
    A. The need for vegetarian food
    B. The need for a carnival
    C. The need for a zoo
    D. The need for a television

11. **What does McMurphy bet he can hit in the cafeteria with a stick of butter?**
    A. Nurse Ratched
    B. Harding
    C. The clock
    D. The server

12. **What does Bromden believe the Catholic nurse tries to rub off like a bad stain?**
    A. Her birthmark
    B. The food that dropped on her clothes
    C. Her tattoo of her ex-boyfriend
    D. Her cigarette habit

13. **Why does Nurse Ratched bring McMurphy back down from the Shock Shop?**
    A. He is enjoying the shocks
    B. He is breaking the machine
    C. He is becoming a legend in the ward
    D. He is losing his mind

14. **Who is the only person with whom Chief Bromden speaks?**
    A. Nurse Ratched
    B. Harding
    C. McMurphy
    D. Dr. Spivey

15. **What is the drug that Sefel refuses to take because it rots his gums?**
    A. Prozac
    B. Cocaine
    C. Dilantin
    D. Wellbutrin

16. **What is the term "chabobs" used to refer to?**
    A. Nurse Ratched's breasts
    B. The inmates' toothpaste
    C. Chief Bromden's deafness
    D. The broken window

17. **Who spies on Nurse Ratched's and the Doctors' meeting about McMurphy?**
    A. Harding
    B. Bibbitt
    C. McMurphy
    D. Chief Bromden

18. **Who is not an Acute?**
    A. Harding
    B. Bibbitt
    C. McMurphy
    D. Chief Bromden

19. **According to Bromden, EST was first tested on what animals?**
    A. Mice
    B. Pigs
    C. Rats
    D. Cows

20. **What is the name of the feared floor where disobedient inmates are sent?**
    A. Red Cross
    B. Public Relation
    C. EST
    D. Disturbed

21. **What is Dilantin used to control?**
    A. Vomiting
    B. Seizures
    C. Heart arrhythmia
    D. Depression

22. **When was One Flew Over the Cuckoo's Nest published?**
    A. 1952
    B. 1962
    C. 1972
    D. 1982

23. **Kesey developed the novel when he was working at which university hospital?**
    A. Harvard
    B. Cornell
    C. Columbia
    D. Stanford

24. **What was Kesey's group of followers known as?**
    A. The Merry Pranksters
    B. The Hallway Men
    C. The Broken Records
    D. The Counterculture Rebels

25. **Kesey's own hallucinations, some of which inspired the novel, came from his use of what?**
    A. Heroin
    B. Cocaine
    C. LSD
    D. Marijuana

Quiz 3 Answer Key

1. **(A)** Order him a lobotomy
2. **(D)** Public Relation
3. **(D)** The music
4. **(B)** Billy's mother
5. **(D)** Chief Bromden
6. **(D)** Posts scary articles about fishing disasters
7. **(A)** Whores
8. **(D)** McMurphy
9. **(C)** Public Relation
10. **(B)** The need for a carnival
11. **(C)** The clock
12. **(A)** Her birthmark
13. **(C)** He is becoming a legend in the ward
14. **(C)** McMurphy
15. **(C)** Dilantin
16. **(A)** Nurse Ratched's breasts
17. **(D)** Chief Bromden
18. **(D)** Chief Bromden
19. **(D)** Cows
20. **(D)** Disturbed
21. **(B)** Seizures
22. **(B)** 1962
23. **(D)** Stanford
24. **(A)** The Merry Pranksters
25. **(C)** LSD

Quiz 4

1. **What is the name of the Catholic nurse so afraid of her own sexuality?**
    A. Nurse Harding
    B. Nurse Bibbitt
    C. Nurse Radon
    D. Nurse Pilbow

2. **Who commits suicide by cutting off his own testicles?**
    A. Rawler
    B. Harding
    C. Bromden
    D. Bibbit

3. **Who is the oldest Chronic in the ward?**
    A. McMurphy
    B. Colonel Matterson
    C. Bibbit
    D. Chief Bromden

4. **Which of these characters does not die?**
    A. Rawler
    B. Bibbitt
    C. Cheswick
    D. Chief Bromden

5. **After electroshock treatment, what does Ellis become?**
    A. An Acute
    B. A doctor
    C. A Chronic
    D. A suicide

6. **Who takes the medication that Sefelt refuses?**
    A. Frederickson
    B. Harding
    C. Bromden
    D. McMurphy

7. **What is the name of the prostitute from Portland whom McMurphy brings to the ward?**
    A. Lady Jane
    B. Ratched Up
    C. Candy Starr
    D. Oceania Aleva

8. **Who is the night watchman on the ward?**
    A. McMurphy
    B. Mr. Turkle
    C. Dr. Spivey
    D. Black Washington

9. **What is the name of Chief Bromden's father?**
    A. The Pine That Stands Tallest
    B. The Cedar of the Holy Trinity
    C. The Mountain on the Bridge
    D. The Oak That Breaks the Wind

10. **Whom does Warren side with in his daily activities?**
    A. Nurse Ratched
    B. McMurphy
    C. Dr. Spivey
    D. Chief Bromden

11. **Why does Sandy not attend the fishing trip?**
    A. She no longer gets along with Candy
    B. McMurphy forgets to pay her
    C. She has gotten married
    D. She broke her foot

12. **Who is the president of the Patients' Council?**
    A. Harding
    B. Bibbitt
    C. Bromden
    D. McMurphy

13. **Why is George nicknamed Rub-a-dub-George?**
    A. Because he drowns in the tub
    B. Because he loses his ring in the pond
    C. Because of his obsession with cleanliness
    D. Because he likes to glug

14. **Who suffers punishment because he asks the purpose of his medications?**
    A. Rawler
    B. Cheswick
    C. McMurphy
    D. Taber

15. **Chief Bromden has what racial background?**
    A. Half Black
    B. Half Asian
    C. Half Turkish
    D. Half Native American

16. **Who is the only other patient who is involuntarily committed beside McMurphy?**
    A. Ratched
    B. Harding
    C. Bibbitt
    D. Scanlon

17. **Who just keeps saying "fuck da wife" over and over?**
    A. Nurse Ratched
    B. Harding
    C. Bibbitt
    D. Ruckley

18. **Who is not one of Nurse Ratched's boys?**
    A. Geever
    B. Rawler
    C. Warren
    D. Washington

19. Who claims he was tired of life?

    A. Bancini

    B. Harding

    C. Bibbitt

    D. Dr. Spivey

20. What is McMurphy's full name?

    A. Hallo McMurphy

    B. A.F. McMurphy

    C. G.S. McMurphy

    D. R.P. McMurphy

21. What does a lobotomy entail?

    A. Removal of a brain lobe

    B. Removal of an esophagus

    C. Removal of a liver

    D. Removal of a kidney

22. Who does Candy Starr have sex with on the last night?

    A. Harding

    B. Bromden

    C. McMurphy

    D. Bibbit

23. Whom does Miss Flinn discuss McMurphy with?

    A. Nurse Ratched

    B. Red Cross Nurse

    C. Dr. Spivey

    D. Public Relation

24. What is the first name of Harding's wife?

    A. Pilbow

    B. Greever

    C. Grayley

    D. Vera

25. **How does Cheswick die?**
    A. Drowning in the pool
    B. Slitting his throat
    C. Drowning in an outside pond
    D. Cutting off his testicles

Quiz 4 Answer Key

1. **(D)** Nurse Pilbow
2. **(A)** Rawler
3. **(B)** Colonel Matterson
4. **(D)** Chief Bromden
5. **(C)** A Chronic
6. **(A)** Frederickson
7. **(C)** Candy Starr
8. **(B)** Mr. Turkle
9. **(A)** The Pine That Stands Tallest
10. **(A)** Nurse Ratched
11. **(C)** She has gotten married
12. **(A)** Harding
13. **(C)** Because of his obsession with cleanliness
14. **(D)** Taber
15. **(D)** Half Native American
16. **(D)** Scanlon
17. **(D)** Ruckley
18. **(B)** Rawler
19. **(A)** Bancini
20. **(D)** R.P. McMurphy
21. **(A)** Removal of a brain lobe
22. **(D)** Bibbit
23. **(A)** Nurse Ratched
24. **(D)** Vera
25. **(A)** Drowning in the pool

ClassicNotes

GradeSaver™

Getting you the grade since 1999™

Other ClassicNotes from GradeSaver™

1984
Absalom, Absalom
Adam Bede
The Adventures of Augie
   March
The Adventures of
   Huckleberry Finn
The Adventures of Tom
   Sawyer
The Aeneid
Agamemnon
The Age of Innocence
The Alchemist
Alice in Wonderland
All My Sons
All Quiet on the Western
   Front
All the King's Men
All the Pretty Horses
The Ambassadors
American Beauty
Angela's Ashes
Animal Farm
Anna Karenina
Antigone
Antony and Cleopatra
Aristotle's Ethics
Aristotle's Poetics
Aristotle's Politics
As I Lay Dying
As You Like It
Astrophil and Stella
The Awakening
Babbitt
The Bacchae
Bartleby the Scrivener

The Bean Trees
The Bell Jar
Beloved
Benito Cereno
Beowulf
Bhagavad-Gita
Billy Budd
Black Boy
Bleak House
The Bloody Chamber
Bluest Eye
The Bonfire of the
   Vanities
The Book of the Duchess
   and Other Poems
Brave New World
Breakfast at Tiffany's
The Brothers Karamazov
Call of the Wild
Candide
The Canterbury Tales
Cat's Cradle
Catch-22
The Catcher in the Rye
The Caucasian Chalk
   Circle
The Cherry Orchard
The Chosen
A Christmas Carol
Chronicle of a Death
   Foretold
Civil Disobedience
Civilization and Its
   Discontents
A Clockwork Orange
The Color of Water

The Color Purple
Comedy of Errors
Communist Manifesto
A Confederacy of
   Dunces
Confessions
Connecticut Yankee in
   King Arthur's Court
The Consolation of
   Philosophy
Coriolanus
The Count of Monte
   Cristo
Crime and Punishment
The Crucible
Cry, the Beloved
   Country
The Crying of Lot 49
Cymbeline
Daisy Miller
Death in Venice
Death of a Salesman
The Death of Ivan Ilych
Democracy in America
Devil in a Blue Dress
Dharma Bums
The Diary of a Young
   Girl by Anne Frank
Disgrace
Divine Comedy-I:
   Inferno
A Doll's House
Don Quixote Book I
Don Quixote Book II
Dr. Faustus
Dr. Jekyll and Mr. Hyde

For our full list of over 250 Study Guides, Quizzes,
Sample College Application Essays, Literature Essays and E-texts, visit:

www.gradesaver.com

ClassicNotes

GrAdeSaver™

Getting you the grade since 1999™

Other ClassicNotes from GradeSaver™

Dracula
Dubliners
East of Eden
The Electric Kool-Aid Acid Test
Emma
Ender's Game
Endgame
The English Patient
Ethan Frome
The Eumenides
Everything is Illuminated
Fahrenheit 451
The Fall of the House of Usher
Farewell to Arms
The Federalist Papers
For Whom the Bell Tolls
The Fountainhead
Frankenstein
Franny and Zooey
Glass Menagerie
The God of Small Things
The Good Earth
The Grapes of Wrath
Great Expectations
The Great Gatsby
The Guest
Gulliver's Travels
Hamlet
The Handmaid's Tale
Hard Times
Heart of Darkness
Hedda Gabler
Henry IV (Pirandello)
Henry IV Part 1

Henry IV Part 2
Henry V
Herzog
The Hobbit
Homo Faber
House of Mirth
House of the Seven Gables
The House of the Spirits
House on Mango Street
Howards End
A Hunger Artist
I Know Why the Caged Bird Sings
An Ideal Husband
Iliad
The Importance of Being Earnest
In Our Time
Inherit the Wind
Invisible Man
The Island of Dr. Moreau
Jane Eyre
Jazz
The Jew of Malta
The Joy Luck Club
Julius Caesar
Jungle of Cities
Kama Sutra
Kidnapped
King Lear
The Kite Runner
Last of the Mohicans
Leviathan
Libation Bearers
Life is Beautiful

Light In August
The Lion, the Witch and the Wardrobe
Lolita
Long Day's Journey Into Night
Lord Jim
Lord of the Flies
The Lord of the Rings: The Fellowship of the Ring
The Lord of the Rings: The Return of the King
The Lord of the Rings: The Two Towers
A Lost Lady
Love in the Time of Cholera
The Love Song of J. Alfred Prufrock
Lucy
Macbeth
Madame Bovary
Manhattan Transfer
Mansfield Park
MAUS
The Mayor of Casterbridge
Measure for Measure
Medea
Merchant of Venice
Metamorphoses
The Metamorphosis
Middlemarch

For our full list of over 250 Study Guides, Quizzes,
Sample College Application Essays, Literature Essays and E-texts, visit:

www.gradesaver.com

ClassicNotes

GradeSaver™

Getting you the grade since 1999™

Other ClassicNotes from GradeSaver™

Things Fall Apart
The Threepenny Opera
Thus Spoke Zarathustra
The Time Machine
Titus Andronicus
To Build a Fire
To Kill a Mockingbird
To the Lighthouse
Treasure Island
Troilus and Cressida
Turn of the Screw
Twelfth Night
Ulysses
Uncle Tom's Cabin
Utopia
A Very Old Man With
   Enormous Wings
Villette
The Visit
Volpone
Waiting for Godot
Waiting for Lefty
Walden
Washington Square
The Waste Land
Where the Red Fern
   Grows
White Fang
White Noise
White Teeth
Who's Afraid of Virginia
   Woolf
Wide Sargasso Sea
Winesburg, Ohio
The Winter's Tale
The Woman Warrior

Wordsworth's Poetical
   Works
Woyzeck
Wuthering Heights
The Yellow Wallpaper
Yonnondio: From the
   Thirties

For our full list of over 250 Study Guides, Quizzes,
Sample College Application Essays, Literature Essays and E-texts, visit:

www.gradesaver.com

Made in the USA
Middletown, DE
23 September 2020